CONTENTS

1)	Introduction To Aristophanes	1
2)	Introduction to The Comic Drama	3
3)	The Acharnians	11
4)	The Knights	22
5)	The Clouds	28
6)	The Wasps	36
7)	Peace	45
8)	The Birds	54
9)	Lysistrata	63
10)	The Thesmophiazusae	74
11)	The Frogs	82
12)	The Ecclesiazusae	92

13)	Plutus	100
14)	Essay Questions and Answers	110
15)	Bibliography	114

BRIGHT NOTES

THE PLAYS OF ARISTOPHANES

Intelligent Education

Nashville, Tennessee

BRIGHT NOTES: The Plays of Aristophanes
www.BrightNotes.com

No part of this publication may be used or reproduced in any manner whatsoever without written permission, except in the case of brief quotations in critical articles and reviews. For permissions, contact Influence Publishers http://www.influencepublishers.com.

ISBN: 978-1-645424-42-0 (Paperback)
ISBN: 978-1-645424-43-7 (eBook)

Published in accordance with the U.S. Copyright Office Orphan Works and Mass Digitization report of the register of copyrights, June 2015.

Originally published by Monarch Press.
H Richmond Neuville, 1966
2020 Edition published by Influence Publishers.

Interior design by Lapiz Digital Services. Cover Design by Thinkpen Designs.

Printed in the United States of America.

Library of Congress Cataloging-in-Publication Data forthcoming.
Names: Intelligent Education
Title: BRIGHT NOTES: The Plays of Aristophanes
Subject: STU004000 STUDY AIDS / Book Notes

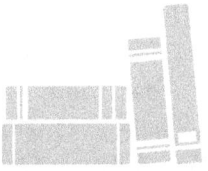

INTRODUCTION TO ARISTOPHANES

Aristophanes was born between 450 and 444 B.C., the son of Philippos, in the Athenian deme of Kudathenaion. This deme is outside the city of Athens, so Aristophanes was mainly raised in a country atmosphere which was in contrast to the effeminate and sophistic climate of the city. His family must have been cultured, for Aristophanes shows a fine knowledge of Greek literature. While he was a teen-ager, the Peloponnesian War between Athens and Sparta, and their allies, began. In 427, Aristophanes produced his Daitales against the city climate and culture which he thought unmanly. It won a second prize. The following year, he produced The Babylonians at the Festival of the Great Dionysia, in which he attacked all the authorities in Athens, but particularly Cleon. Both of these plays were presented under the name of Callistratus. Cleon objected to The Babylonians, since the audience contained foreigners, and he prosecuted Aristophanes for treason. Fortunately, Aristophanes escaped.

In 425, Aristophanes produced *The Acharnians* under his own name, and it won first prize at the Lenaean Festival. The next year, he produced *The Knights*, which also won the first prize at the Lenaea. This was followed in 423 by the lost Holkades, presented at the Lenaea, and *The Clouds*, which won the third (and last) prize at the Great Dionysia. In 422, Aristophanes attacked the juries' savagery in *The Wasps,* winning second prize at the Festival of the Lenaea, and produced the Georgi, probably at the Great Dionysia. That autumn, Cleon died. In 421, Aristophanes' *Peace* won the second prize at the Great Dionysia, produced just before the Peace of Nicias was signed. It is thought that the Geras, on old age, was produced between 421 and 414. In 414, Aristophanes produced the Amphiaraus at the Lenaea and *The Birds* at the Great Dionysia, for which he won second prize.

In 411, *Lysistrata,* one of Aristophanes' best-known plays, was presented at the Lenaea. The next year saw the first production of the *Thesmophoriazusae,* probably at the Lenaean Festival. In 408, Aristophanes produced the first version of *Plutus*, and the *Thesmophoriazusae* in its present version, as well as the *Triphales.* During this period he also wrote the *Lemniai*, the *Gerytades*, and the *Phoenissae.* The only plays surviving are *Lysistrata* and the second version of the *Thesmophoriazusae.* During this same period, in 406, the tragedians Euripides and Sophocles died.

In 405, Aristophanes produced the prize-winning *The Frogs* at the Lenaea, as well as the *Niobos.* After a hiatus until 392, Aristophanes' next known play was produced. But this interval witnessed the Fall of Athens in 404, the changes in types of government in Athens, and the trial and death of Socrates (399 B.C.). In 392, *The Ecclesiazusae* was produced in **parody** of Plato's Republic. In 388, the new version of *Plutus* was produced. After this date, we know only that Aristophanes produced the Kokalus and the Aiolosikon. He is generally believed to have died in 388 B.C.

INTRODUCTION TO THE COMIC DRAMA

ORIGINS

According to Aristotle's Poetics, Greek poetry derives from imitation and the delight in imitation. Poetry, however, soon broke up into two kinds: graver poets would represent noble actions, and those of noble persons; meaner poets would represent the actions of the ignoble. The first is tragic drama, the second comic drama. Aristotle's discussion of tragic and **epic** poetry is contained in his Poetics, that of comedy in a lost second book to the Poetics. From what we have, however, we can deduce that comedy was considered by Aristotle to deal with the lower classes of society. This division was carried on in the Renaissance to include the following characteristics:

1. The characters of tragedy are kings, princes, or great leaders; those of comedy are humble and private citizens.

2. Tragedy deals with great and terrible actions, while comedy deals with familiar and domestic actions.

3. Tragedy begins happily and progresses to a terrible ending, but comedy begins rather turbulently and ends joyfully.

4. The style and language of tragedy are elevated and sublime, while those of comedy are humble and colloquial.

5. Tragedy generally deals with historical subjects; comedy deals with invented situations.

6. Tragedy deals with exile and bloodshed, but comedy deals largely with love and seduction.

When we compare these criteria to Aristophanic comedy, we find that Old Comedy's characters are humble people or private citizens; the actions are sometimes domestic, but often they have important and great meanings; comedy ends happily, usually in a festival; the style is humble and the **diction** is not only colloquial but obscene; comedy deals with fantastic, invented situations, but also with contemporary problems disguised by surface fantasy; and love and seduction are incidental and a small part of Aristophanic comedy.

Comedy ultimately derives from the komoidia, the song of the komos or revel, particularly the revels which took place at the festivals of Dionysus, the god of the vine and, more importantly, of fertility. According to Aristotle, comedy's origin is with the leaders of the phallic performances. The phallic komos developed in primitive times when it was discovered that the phallus and the female genitalia were directly related to the production of children. Even today, for example, the Australian aborigine believes that reproduction occurs from the influence of particular nature and totem spirits, not from sexual intercourse. The phallic ceremony took place at festivals, particularly those of Demeter (a grain goddess) and Dionysus (the god of the vine), and it consisted of a religious procession of the revelers and dancing and singing to ensure the fertility of the crops. Occasionally, the phallic rite included intercourse in the fields so that the fertility of the participants might affect the fertility of the land.

Old Comedy, or Aristophanic Comedy, modifies the ritual into art. But Aristophanic Comedy still retained vestiges of the old ritual. The phallus plays a prominent part in the costuming and staging of the play; the play ends generally in a gamos or festive union of the sexes, either at a party or in marriages; and the off-color references to male or female genitalia are not so much obscene as carry-overs of the old ritual. With later Aristophanic Comedy, these elements tend to disappear or be played down.

In 486 B.C. comedy was officially recognized in Athens and became a part of the Dionysian celebrations at the Great Dionysia as well as the less formal lenaea. By the time Aristophanes wrote his first play, Old Comedy was well established, but the only examples that have survived are the first nine of Aristophanes' eleven extant plays.

THE THEATER

Both tragedies and comedies were presented in the open-air theater (theatron or koilon), semi-circular in shape. Tiers of seats ranged upward from the lowest seats, frequently taking advantage of sloping ground to form a natural amphitheater. Their size attests the popularity of drama: the Theater of Dionysus in Athens could seat 17,000. In fact, the Greeks invented the theater building.

A flat place at the bottom of the hillside was circumscribed by a circle on which was constructed the orchestra, where the chorus danced and performed. In its center was an altar to Dionysus which was also used as a stage property in many plays. Facing the altar, in the first row center, sat the priest of Dionysus. Forming the flat end of the semi-circular orchestra was the skene ("tent" or "hut" from which we have the word "scene"). It was a wooden or stone structure which could represent the front of a house, palace, temple, or row of houses. Most of the action occurred on a low platform at its base (the proskenion). The three doors of the skene were used for the actor's entrance or exit, as required. The skene itself was used inside for the actors' dressing room. The Chorus did not enter through the skene, but from entrances on both sides called the parodoi. The orchestra was used for the opening prayers of the festival, as well as the choral dances and whatever action might require the actors to move forward. The top of the skene was also used for scenes set on the roof of a building. From there descended the deux ex machina ("god from a machine") which Aristophanes used for the passage of gods, for Socrates' basket, and for Trygaeus; ascent to heaven. Since gods were expected to descend from above, it was necessary to have a mechanical contrivance (also called the "machine") to lower them to the acting area. The device is, of course, less important than the dramatic use made of it.

Another important stage device was the eccyclema, a platform which could be rotated or rolled out to reveal a scene inside the house. Euripides, for instance, appears to Dicaeopolis in *The Acharnians* in an eccyclema.

As drama became more established, two wings were added to each side of the skene to frame the acting area. These are the paraskene ("beside the skene").

OCCASIONS FOR THE DRAMA

Plays were primarily produced at the Great Dionysia, held in March to April, in Athens, for the Festival of Dionysus. This feast was originally reserved for tragedy, but eventually came to include three days of tragic production and one day of comedies. The tragedians had to present four plays, three of them tragedies, and the fourth a lighter piece, usually a satyr play. The satyr play derived its name from the Chorus, which always consisted of satyrs. The satyrs were mythological attendants of Dionysus, and were represented as men with pointed ears, short horns, and goat legs. The three tragedies might or might not be related to one another. At the beginning of tragic production, this "trilogy" did revolve around a common story. By the time of Sophocles and Euripides, a common motif was no longer required. The satyr plays were offered as a light diversion after a day-long attendance at the theater, seated on hard benches. Three tragedians competed for prizes, each presenting a set of three tragedies and a satyr play on each day. Comedies were submitted singly by three playwrights on the fourth day, also in competition for a prize for comedy.

Comedy was the production staged at the Festival of the Lenaea ("Wine Press"), held January to February. A third festival was the Rural Dionysia held between December and January in various towns within the Greek peninsula.

DRAMATIC PRODUCTION

All plays were presented during the day, thus very rarely does the action call for a night scene. The actors themselves were always men and always wore masks so that everyone could readily recognize the type of character or characteristic being portrayed. The number of speaking actors on stage at any one time did not exceed three, for the individual actors would change masks and costumes off-stage and re-enter as a different character. A certain larger-than-life appearance was given the actor by the use of the cothurnus, the high-soled boot. Comic actors customarily wore a short tunic which could expose the large phallus each carried. Since the roles of women in Aristophanic comedy were played by men, it is obvious that the nude or exposed women in the plays are really costumed representations of the female body.

STRUCTURE OF COMEDY

Unlike Greek Tragedy, Old Comedy has a typical plot which has an organic relationship with its formal structure.

Prologue

In the Prologue, the leading character conceives a "happy idea," extravagantly imaginative or absurdly impractical, which will solve some problem.

Parodos

The entrance of the Chorus, which frequently personifies non-humans such as clouds, wasps, frogs, etc.

Agon

The debate in which the "happy idea" is opposed and defended, thus establishing the main subject of the play. Those opposed to the idea are always defeated.

Parabasis

The actors retire and the Chorus comes forward to address the audience directly. The Chorus expresses the poet's ideas on a variety of subjects, and normally states the **theme** of the play and its implications in plain language. Occasionally the Chorus defends the playwright.

Episodes

In the episodes, the "happy idea" is put into practice. The consequences of the idea are dramatized in a series of scenes, interrupted by stasima or choral songs commenting on the scene, which show the leading character and typical figures who would be affected by the idea. The **episodes** usually have no sequential connection with each other; they do tend, however, to rise to an emotional climax.

Exodos

Plays frequently end with a feast or some form of male-female union (the gamos), as might be expected from plays originating in a fertility rite.

SUBJECT MATTER OF THE COMEDIES

In general, it might be said that comedy strives to be as different as possible from tragedy. Dignity becomes frivolity; reason becomes absurdity; morality becomes license. Yet there is a constant seriousness in the trenchant political **satire**; and closely associated with the political satire is personal abuse directed to specific individuals. Frank to the point of shocking prudes, this abuse is usually obscene and frequently unfair. Obscenity and earthy humor are favorite devices in Old Comedy. The characters of the author's invention, as well as the gods and heroes from mythology, are shown as low-comedy types. A further contribution to the general air of incongruity of the elements of Old Comedy is the supremely beautiful poetry of Aristophanes, which includes some of the finest lyrics ever written.

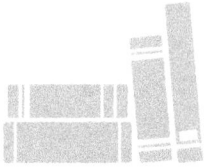

ARISTOPHANES

THE ACHARNIANS

BACKGROUND

The Acharnians concerns the "men of Acharnae," a deme seven miles to the north of Athens. It was the third play written by the young Aristophanes - the first two are lost - under the pseudonym of Callistratus. This play, written seven years after the Peloponnesian War began and five years after Pericles' death, is a political play urging the Athenians to make peace with the Spartans. *The Acharnians* won first prize at the Festival of Lenaea in 425 B.C.

CHARACTERS

Dicaeopolis: "Just city," the model of the good citizen of Athens who desires peace with the Spartans.

Herald

Amphitheus: Dicaeopolis' friend and aid.

Pseudartabas: "False Measure," the Persian Ambassador.

Theorus

Daughter Of Dicaeopolis

Euripides: The Greek tragedian.

Euripides' Slave

Lamachus: An Athenian general who represents the war party in Athens.

A Megarian

His Two Daughters

An Informer

A Boeotian

Nicarchus

Lamachus' Slave

A Husbandman

A Wedding Guest

Ambassadors

Chorus Of Acharnian Coal-Burners

PROLOGUE

Dicaeopolis is seated alone in the Pynx waiting for the assembly of Pyrtanes to arrive. He complains that they never trouble themselves about peace, and regrets that he gave up his country life for the city. The Pyrtanes enter and Amphitheus, a citizen, rises to speak. Although he is a descendant of a god and therefore immortal, he is hungry. The assembly herald calls the police to remove Amphitheus, but Dicaeopolis objects that it is an outrage: Amphitheus only desired to secure peace from the war. The herald ignores Dicaeopolis' demand to speak of peace and announces the ambassadors, just returned from the Great King. While they discourse on the hardships of their mission, living for eleven years in luxury in Persia, Dicaeopolis delivers sarcastic "asides" on them. The Persian ambassador, Pseudartabas, enters, accompanied by two eunuchs. He speaks incomprehensibly, and the ambassadors say that the Great King will send Athens gold. Pseudartabas then plainly says that the Athenians will get no gold. The ambassadors persist in interpreting Pseudartabas' remarks favorably, and after a few nasty remarks, Dicaeopolis leaves the Pynx in disgust. He gets in touch with Amphitheus and gives him eight drachma to conclude a private truce with the Spartans.

Dicaeopolis returns to the assembly and hears Theorus, the Athenian ambassador to Thrace, reporting. The Thracians have sent the most warlike soldiers in all Thrace to help the Athenians. The Thracian "soldiers" enter and are seen to be unwarlike in appearance and circumcised. While Dicaeopolis argues against these mercenaries they steal his sack of garlic. Dicaeopolis opposes paying the Thracians and objects to his mistreatment by barbarians. Besides, he has just felt a drop of rain. The herald declares that the assembly is over until two days later. Dicaeopolis is alone in the Pynx when Amphitheus returns. Amphitheus was intercepted by some old men from Acharnae, who fought at Marathon. They oppose peace because the Spartans recently cut their grape vine. Amphitheus brings three kinds of treaties from the Spartans: a five-year, a ten-year, and a thirty-year treaty. Each is in a bottle. Dicaeopolis doesn't like the taste of the first two bottles, but the thirty-year bottle is delicious. He is free of the war and will celebrate the rural Dionysia.

Comment

The Assembly seems to have always started late. Dicaeopolis' proposal for peace is voiced by Amphitheus, whose idea is rejected. Dicaeopolis is disgusted and abandons the city, despite his name. His commitment to peace entails an abandonment of the polis which has accepted the false Persian and ignored justice. The ambassadors have spent more time in luxurious living than in accomplishing their mission. Peace as liquors is a consistent image, culminating in the Exodos.

PARODOS

The Chorus of Acharnian Coal-Burners enters in the empty Pynx. They are the Acharnians who have been following Amphitheus. They want the war to continue and have no mercy for their foes. In fact, they will delight in stoning the pacifist.

AGON

Within his house, Dicaeopolis yells at them, "Peace! Profane men!" He comes out, followed by his wife and two daughters.

Two slaves carry a ritual phallus. Dicaeopolis carries a pot and sings a hymn to Phales in honor of the peace. The Acharnians rush out and try to stone him for treason in concluding a peace with the Spartans. They hate Dicaeopolis worse than Cleon. Dicaeopolis tries to explain the reasons he concluded the peace treaty, but the Acharnians refuse to listen; they want to stone him. Dicaeopolis says, "Very well," but he has their fellow-citizen. He goes back into his house and returns with a basket of Acharnian coals. If they stone him, he will dismember their coals. They drop their stones and agree to listen to Dicaeopolis' arguments. Before he will speak, however, he recalls his terrible treatment the year before when Cleon dragged him before the Senate because of his comedy. He almost perished. Now he desires to dress in a manner that will be likely to draw pity.

Comment

Dicaeopolis and his family celebrate a phallic feast to Dionysus, in honor of fertility, in contrast to the sterility and futility of war. Aristophanes refers to his Babylonians.

Dicaeopolis goes to Euripides' house and knocks on the door. The slave tells him that Euripides is and is not at home. He is physically there, but mentally not there, for he is composing a tragedy. Euripides is disclosed in his upstairs room composing a new tragedy. Dicaeopolis remarks that he might just as well write them on the ground: his heroes dress like beggars. He asks for a ragged costume in which to address the chorus. Euripides offers him the costumes of Oneus, Phoenix, Philoctetes, Bellerophon, and Telephus. Dicaeopolis takes the rags of Telephus; they are tattered enough to dupe the chorus. He also begs for a beggar's staff and a basket with a lamp lighted inside it. Euripides gives him these accessories and chases him away from the house. But he also wants a little broken cup and a little pot with a sponge. He hopes that Euripides' destiny will be as brilliant as his mother's. Euripides replies that Dicaepolis is stealing a whole tragedy. Dicaeopolis has one further request: would Euripides give him some herbs for the basket? After he gets the herbs, he returns again to beg some chervil that Euripides' mother let him in a will. Euripides chases him out and locks the door.

Comment

Aristophanes never stopped mocking Euripides for his low tragic characters and because his mother sold vegetables. Euripides was also a leader in introducing the new rhetoric and oratorical skills into his plays. Euripides' appearance is managed by the Eccyclema, which rolls out to disclose him "inside" the house.

Dicaeopolis addresses the audience. He begs them not to be angered if he is a beggar, for only in a comedy can what is right be sometimes discerned. In addition, Cleon could not accuse him of denouncing Athens before strangers; the spectators are Athenians at the Festival of Lenaea. Some wretches lost in vice had been denouncing Megarian produce before it was declared contraband. The real conflict, moreover, derived from the Athenians' abduction of the Megarian harlot Simaetha, and the Megarians' reprisal of abducting two harlots from the house of Aspasia. That was when Pericles banished the Megarians and caused the war. The Megarians were dying of hunger and asked the Spartans to abolish the decree. Since then, Athens has been a wartime city. The Chorus divides into two camps which begin to attack one another, some condemning and some agreeing with Dicaeopolis. Lamachus, the Athenian general, rushes out fully armed to help the Chorus. Dicaeopolis asks him to get rid of his weapons; they make him dizzy. He also asks for a plume from his helmet, because he wants to make himself vomit in the shield. When Lamachus protests, Dicaeopolis launches into a full-scale denunciation of ambitious and show-off profiteering officers. Lamachus flees from the barrage of words into his house. Dicaeopolis concludes by announcing to the Peloponnesians, Megarians and Boeotians that he is at peace and his market is open to them.

Comment

The real Lamachus was a brave officer and one of those given the responsibility of negotiating and signing the Peace of Nicas in 421 B.C. Aristophanes uses him as a typical soldier, perhaps because "Lamachus" contains the word for battle, mache.

PARABASIS

The Chorus addresses the audience and recounts the good the author of this comedy has done for them. They are praising him because of the slanders and accusations against him. The author has exposed the flatteries of the delegates from other cities so that the Athenians would not be hood-winked by them. He speaks the truth and will lead them to happiness. The only reason the Spartans include the transfer of the island Aegina in their peace offers is to rob Athens of her poet. Honesty and justice fight the poet's cause; he will never be a prostitute to the highest bidder. After invoking the Acharnian Muse, the Chorus reproaches Athens: the old veterans who fought for Athens are ignored. At court, they can only stammer out a few words while they are overwhelmed by the rhetoric of their accusers. It is scandalous and unjust, they conclude, that the aged Thucydides is browbeaten by the young Cephisodemus.

Comment

Thucydides (ca. 460 - ca. 400 B.C.) was the author of a history of the Peloponnesian War. In 424 he was one of ten generals sent to Thrace, but he failed to relieve another general and was sent into exile for twenty years. The implication of Aristophanes' remark is that, while old men are full of warlike spirit and are strict in their decisions, the young men are smooth orators who trick the prisoners into guilt, especially if the prisoners are old, unfamiliar with court practice, or not Athenians.

Episode I

Dicaeopolis opens his market, and his first commerce is with a Megarian trader. The starving Megarian disguises his two daughters as sows and trades them for garlic and salt. The scene is a hilarious one, based on the double meaning of choiros for "sow" and the slang expression for female genitalia. At the end of the **episode**, Dicaeopolis chases off an informer who wants to denounce Athens' enemies.

STASIMON I

The Chorus comments on how happy is Dicaeopolis. Peacefully seated in his market, he is successful in his every wish.

Episode II

A prosperous Boeotian enters the market and offers to sell delicacies and various kinds of birds, animals, fish, and eels. Dicaeopolis takes the eel as a market tax. In exchange for all he has, the Boeotian asks for some Athenian produce they do not have in Boeotia. Dicaeopolis offers him Phaleric anchovies and pottery, but the Boeotian wants an informer. These are in plentiful supply in Athens. Nicarchus, an informer, enters to denounce the contraband from Boeotia. They bind and gag the informer and pack him in a crate like a piece of pottery. The informer is a vase good for all purposes: a vessel for containing all foul things, a mortar to pound law-suits together, a lamp for spying on false accounts, and a cup to mix up and poison everything. After the Boeotian leaves, a slave enters to buy some thrushes and an eel for Lamachus, but Dicaeopolis refuses to give him anything.

STASIMON II

The Chorus points out Dicaeopolis' good fortune and profound wisdom. All good things come unsought to him. The Chorus then denounces war and states that it will never welcome the god of war at its house.

Comment

The Megarian and the Boeotian represent the opposite results of war. The Megarians are starving and destroyed; the Boeotians are spared the hardships of war and prosper (perhaps because they have no informers). Aristophanes attacks the ever-present informers and spies in Athens during the war. War-fever leads to all kinds of corruption and profiteering.

Episode III

A herald enters to announce a drinking contest. While Dicaeopolis gets ready for the feast, a poor husbandman enters to beg part of the peace Dicaeopolis has made. But he refuses to give him even a drop of peace. A wedding guest enters to request a glass of peace for a new bridegroom. Dicaeopolis refuses again to share his peace. Just then the Maid of Honor comes in and whispers in Dicaeopolis' ear. He relents and gives some peace to them. For the bride is a woman and should not suffer from war. She can rub some drops of peace on her husband where it will do the most good. The herald re-enters and informs Lamachus that he has been ordered to go north in the snow to guard the frontier. Dicaeopolis is jeering at Lamachus when another herald approaches and urges him to hurry to the feast. Everyone is waiting for him. Lamachus and Dicaeopolis order their slaves to prepare their provisions, and Lamachus' poor diet contrasts with the delicacies Dicaeopolis has.

STASIMON III

The Chorus comments on the difference in the journeys of Lamachus and Dicaeopolis. Since, when Lamachus was choregus at the Lenaea the audience went away hungry, the Chorus hopes that he will not eat well and will suffer a misfortune.

KOMOS-GAMOS

Lamachus limps in suffering from a spear wound. At the same time Dicaeopolis returns from the feast with two courtesans. He is happy, for he was the first to drain his cup and thus won first prize. While Lamachus tells his soldiers to hold his leg tenderly, Dicaeopolis urges the girls to his penis. He intends to make love tonight. Lamachus is carried off in pain, and the Chorus sings "Triumph" around Dicaeopolis.

Comment

The pacifist ends with a feast and two beautiful girls, while the warmonger is painfully wounded. The play is not only a hilarious **satire** of Athenian legislative follies and Euripides; it is also a political attempt to make the Athenians see the folly of war. That this play was permitted on stage during the war is a tribute to the spirit of Athens in the fifth century. No modern country would permit such open, comic abuse of its leaders and policies during similar circumstances.

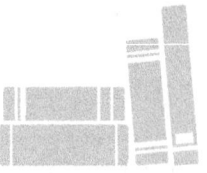

ARISTOPHANES

THE KNIGHTS

BACKGROUND

The Knights also won the first prize for Aristophanes, and this time a play was produced under his own name. Of the eleven extant plays of Aristophanes, however, this one is the poorest. It lacks humorous **episodes** and taste, and is more of an attack on Cleon than anything else. It is juvenile and vitriolic, with only a few small scenes of any worth.

CHARACTERS

Demosthenes and Nicias: Servants of Demos.

Agroacritus: A Sausage-seller.

Cleon: The Athenian ruler.

Demos: A personification of the Athenian people.

Chorus of Knights

PROLOGUE

Demosthenes and Nicias enter the Pynx, complaining about a new Paphlagonian slave who has entered their master's house. Their master Demos is brutal and bad-tempered. He recently bought as a slave of Paphlagonian who is a rogue and the personification of calumny. He butters up their master and extorts contributions from the other slaves. Demosthenes and Nicias determine to find some way of doing away with the Paphlagonian.

After drinking wine to improve his thinking, Demosthenes tells Nicias to steal the Paphlagonian's oracles. They read the oracles that the governing of the city will be directed first by a dealer in oakum, next by a sheep-dealer, and then the Paphlagonian until a filthier scoundrel arises. Demosthenes and Nicias decide to get a sausage-dealer to overthrow their tormenter. Agoracritus is just passing by on his way to the market, and they persuade him that he is the one destined to be the next ruler of Athens. Agoracritus' illiteracy is no problem: "A demagogue must be neither an educated nor an honest man; he has to be an ignoramus and a rogue." Governing people, moreover, is the same as making sausages.

Mix and knead together all the state business as you do for sausages. To win the people, always cook them some savory that pleases them. Besides, you possess all the attributes of a demogogue; a screeching, horrible voice, a perverse, cross-grained nature and the language of the market-place. In you all is united which is needful for governing.

Cleon, the Paphlagonian, comes out and discovers the conspirators. But Demosthenes calls for the knights to defend them.

Comment

Demosthenes and Nicias were the Athenian generals in command of the attack on the Spartan island of Sphacteria in 425 B.C. Their efforts were slow, and Cleon denounced their incompetence in the Assembly. He boasted that he could capture the Spartans in twenty days. Nicias resigned, and Cleon was forced to make good his boast. Fortunately, a forest fire destroyed all the cover on the island. Cleon thus captured and destroyed the Spartans in twenty days and returned to Athens in triumph, more powerful than before. Aristpohanes immediately attacked the successful Cleon in this, his next play. Cleon, however, was so powerful that it is said that the mask-makers refused to make a mask for the character of Cleon. It is also reported that Aristophanes played the part of Cleon himself.

PARODOS

The knights enter quickly and begin to attack Cleon. Cleon is called a villain, a public robber, a yawning gulf of plunder.

PROAGON

Cleon bawls incessantly and calls for help. But the sausage-dealer can yell louder and denounce him. The two engage in a vituperative name-calling battle. Demosthenes and the Chorus participate, attacking Cleon's impudence and evil. At the end of the brawl, Cleon runs out to the Senate to reveal the conspiracy.

PARABASIS

The Chorus explains to the audience why the poet has not before presented a play under his name. It is because the comic muse is difficult to court, and because the Athenians are fickle by nature and abandon their poets when they grow old. Magnes, Cratinus, Connas, and Crates are forgotten in their old age. The poet, moreover, has been cautious in his apprenticeship. The Chorus then prays to Poesidon and Athena and praises the past glories of Athens' knights.

Comment

Cleon is attacked for getting money by embezzlement, extortion, or blackmail. The reason he prefers war is that the chaos covers up his evil deeds. Cleon admits the accusations are true; he did it for Demos, the city. In reality, Cleon did keep the deme of Athens from starvation by his policies. Aristophanes' attack on Cleon is directed against his person rather than his policies - the only way Cleon can be deposed from his position of trust in Demos' house is to find someone more vulgar, more corrupt, and a greater impostor.

AGON

The struggle for control of the Senate occurs off-stage, but the sausage-seller relates his victory: when he arrived at the Senate, Cleon had convinced the Senate that the knights were evil. Agoracritus prayed to the gods of rascals and of the market place to give him "unbridled audacity, an untiring chatter and a shameless voice." Right afterwards, a pederast on his right broke wind. After a series of bribes, Agoracritus won the Senate's approval and Cleon was arrested. Cleon suddenly rushes in and begins to berate the sausage-seller, each threatening to maul and maim the other. They decide to go to persuade Demos. They start by praising Demos and fawning on him, telling him how much they love him. Interspersed throughout are vituperative attacks against one another. Then they switch to reading various oracles they have in their possession that are extremely obscure and absurd, each proving that the other is evil. Finally, Agoracritus and Cleon compete in feeding and coddling Demos. After Agoracritus steals Cleon's stewed hare, Demos expels Cleon because Agoracritus is more impudent.

Comment

Pederasty and homosexuality are often mentioned in Greek literature. Cleon, born of the common people, opposed and tried to stop homosexuality in Athens by removing such men from enfranchisement as citizens. Aristophanes shared Cleon's dislike of homosexuals and their effeminacies.

PARABASIS II

The Chorus remarks to the audience that an insult given to the wicked is laudable. The debauched brother of Ariphrades wallows in vice and pollutes his tongue in brothels. Cleonymus is a glutton when he dines with a rich host.

EXODOS

Agoracritus enters and informs the Chorus that Demos is living in ancient Athens. Demos appears and is seen to be rejuvenated and redeemed. Agoracritus reviews Demos' past errors in the Assembly, making him realize how he had been swayed by effeminate and ambitious orators. Agoracritus, moreover, has released Truce from her captivity. Cleon had locked her up in the house so that Demos could not enjoy her. Cleon's punishment will be to sell sausages of asses' and dogs' meat, be continually drunk, exchange foul language with prostitutes, and drink dirty water from the baths.

Comment

The City, figured by Demos, rejects flattery and welfare doles. Demos will no longer use opportunity for profit to sway the juries, and he will reform the military service. Aristophanes' attack on Cleon's war-mania and policy suggests that it is nothing else than the selling of diseased meat, unhealthful and disgusting. Cleon has fallen from a power-hungry ruler to the lowest person in the city.

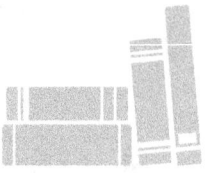

ARISTOPHANES

THE CLOUDS

BACKGROUND

Riding on the wave of success, Aristophanes produced what he thought was his best comedy at the Great Dionysia in 423 B.C. *The Clouds,* however, was too obviously a **didactic** piece, and the Athenians voted it the third and lowest prize. Although the play has fine lyric passages, it is too much a presentation of Aristophanes' educational ideas and his dislike of sophist instruction.

CHARACTERS

Strepsiades: "Twister," an elderly farmer.

Phidippides: "Thrift-Horse," Strepsiades' son.

Strepsiades' Servant

Socrates: The philosopher.

Socrates' Disciples

Just Discourse

Unjust Discourse

Pasias and Amynias: Money lenders.

Chorus Of Clouds

PROLOGUE

A cranky old man, Strepsiades, lies in bed unable to sleep and worrying about the money his son spends on horses. He regrets that he left the country and married a haughty, extravagant woman from the city. When the son was born she wanted him to be named for horsemanship, and they finally called him "Phidippides." Suddenly he has a bright idea and wakes up his son: he will enroll Phidippides in Socrates' Thoughtery. Phidippides objects; they are "quacks with pale faces." Strepsiades wants his son to be able to reason falsely so that he can win law suits, in particular the suits of his creditors against himself. Phidippides again refuses and Strepsiades turns him out of the house.

Strepsiades knocks on the door of The Thoughtery and is berated by a disciple for bringing on the miscarriage of an idea. After warning Strepsiades that these ideas are mysteries, the disciple explains that they were measuring how many times the length of its legs a flea jumps. They also discuss whether a gnat buzzes through its proboscis or its anus, determining that it is through its rump. Strepsiades hears other obscene stories about Socrates' genius and is delighted with his cleverness.

Inside The Thoughtery Strepsiades sees the emaciated disciples of Socrates bent over looking fixedly at the ground. The disciple explains that "they are sounding the abysses of Tartarus," while their rumps "are studying astronomy on their own account." The disciple shows Strepsiades a globe used for astronomy and a map used for geometry.

Strepsiades sees Socrates suspended in a basket, the better to contemplate the sun and penetrate the things of heaven. Strepsiades tells him that he desires to learn how to speak, especially the method of reasoning "whose object is not to repay anything, and, may the gods bear witness, that I am ready to pay any fee you name." Socrates takes Strepsiades in and begins his initiation. He invokes the Clouds, the venerable goddesses and their genii, to come, and Strepsiades covers his head to keep dry.

Comment

The accusation against Socrates that he was impious and taught people to make the worse reason seem the better was current at the end of the fifth century. In fact, the indictment of Socrates in 399 was based on two counts: "Socrates is guilty of not worshipping the gods which the State worships, but introducing new and unfamiliar religious practices; and, further, of corrupting the young."

PARODOS

The Chorus of Clouds enters accompanied by rumblings of thunder. They are the goddesses invoked by Socrates, and Strepsiades lets off his own thunder in greeting them.

AGON

Strepsiades asks Socrates who these women are, and is told that they are "the Clouds of heaven, great goddesses for the lazy; to them we owe all, thoughts, speeches, trickery, roguery, boasting, lies, sagacity." Strepsiades wonders why they look like women. Socrates explains that they change their appearance and take what metamorphosis they like. The Clouds are the only goddesses, all the rest are myth: there is no Zeus. Strepsiades is taken aback, but Socrates proves that rain never appears without the Clouds. Zeus cannot make it rain in a clear sky. Strepsiades replies that the proof is good; he always thought rain came from Zeus urinating into a sieve. Socrates also explains the cause of thunder and lightning.

Soc. Well then, reflect what a noise is produced by your belly, which is but small. Shall not the air, which is boundless, produce these mighty claps of thunder?

Strep. And this is why the names are so much alike: crap and clap.

The Clouds promise to teach Strepsiades great eloquence, and are pleased at his modesty for desiring only "to be able to turn bad law suits to my own advantage and to slip through the fingers of my creditors." To consider Strepsiades' fitness for admission, Socrates takes him into The Thoughtery for an examination. Socrates has doubts because of the stupid and buffoonish comments of Strepsiades.

PARABASIS

The Chorus reviews Aristophanes' career and his previous comedies. Aristophanes, also, presents fresh **themes** and not re-worked one in each play. He attacked Cleon to his face when he was powerful; now that he is fallen, he does not attack him as some of Aristophanes' rivals do. The Chorus points out that the Athenians owe more to the Clouds than to any deity: whenever the Athenians plan some mad expedition, "we thunder or we fall down in rain." When the Clouds were preparing to come to Athens, moreover, the Moon told them that the Athenians treat her shamefully. Although the Moon provides light at night so that the Athenians would not have to pay for candles:

> **Nevertheless you do not reckon the days correctly and your calendar is naught but confusion. Consequently the gods load her with threats when they get home and are disappointed of their meal, because the festival has not been kept in the regular order of time. When you should be sacrificing, you are putting to torture or administering justice.**

Episode I

Socrates bursts out of The Thoughtery, declaring that "I have never seen a man so gross, so inept, so stupid, so forgetful. All the little quibbles, which I teach him, he forgets even before he has learnt them." Socrates hauls Strepsiades outside and tries to instruct him in metrics, but Strepsiades persists in interpreting measure as quantity rather than poetic measure. Socrates tries to teach him the rhythms of poetry, beginning with the dactyl, but Strepsiades makes an obscene gesture with his finger. All Strepsiades wants to learn is "the are of false reasoning." When Socrates tries to teach him the gender of nouns, Strepsiades fails miserably. Strepsiades is told to lie on his bed and think, but all his remarks are about bedbugs. Socrates is finally able to get him to think about schemes for not paying debts, but Strepsiades is so foolish that Socrates chases him out of The Thoughtery.

STASIMON I

The Chorus advises Socrates to take Strepsiades' money, since he is full of admiration and enthusiasm for Socrates.

Comment

The dactyl is a metric foot consisting of a stressed syllable followed by two unstressed syllables (-uu). Strepsiades twists the meaning by confusing the Greek word dakylos (finger) for "dactyl," the measure.

Episode II

Strepsiades pushes his son from the house and tries to teach him some of the things Socrates taught him. There is no Zeus; the Vortex is the supreme deity now. Phidippides thinks it is drivel, but Strepsiades orders him not to insult men who never shave or take a bath in order to economize. He brings his son to The Thoughtery and enrolls him, even though Phidippides warns him that he will regret it. Just and Unjust Discourse come out to teach Phidippides. They are quarreling violently and calling one another names, and the Chorus has to separate them, ordering each to speak in turn. Just Discourse praises the old days of justice and modestly when parents were respected and lewdness avoided. Men were healthy and honorable then. Unjust

Discourse praises the ways to confute the laws by triumphing with weak arguments. How can adultery be enjoyed if the guilty cannot defend themselves? Unjust Discourse wins the argument and takes out Phidippides to educate him.

Comment

Just Discourse argues for the simple, old-fashioned and righteous life. Unjust Discourse argues for skepticism and lax morals, thus taking the position of the new Sophist schools of philosophy and oratory.

PARABASIS II

The Chorus warns the audience to award the play the first prize. The Clouds will rain on the audience's fields first in the spring. If the play does not win the prize, the Clouds threaten them with drought.

Episode II

Several days have passed, and Strepsiades comes back with a present for Socrates. Phidippides has been a great success, and when he comes out he demonstrates that he can argue as technically as the Sophists. Pasias, the moneylender, arrives to collect a debt, but Strepsiades refuses to pay because the man makes a mistake in gender. He also refuses to pay back Amynias, another moneylender, arguing that if the sea doesn't get any fuller with the rivers pouring in, money shouldn't grow either.

STASIMON II

The Chorus warns that this perverse old man will someday be punished for his schemings. He may wish someday that his son did not learn "how to fight against all justice and right and to gain even the most iniquitous causes against his adversaries."

EXODUS

The Chorus has no sooner finished its warnings than Phidippides drives his father out of the house, beating him. Phidippides had defended Euripides as the greatest of poets, but his father said that Euripides' plays are immoral. The son justifies beating his father because the old man is now in his second childhood, and it is lawful for children to be beaten. Strepsiades appeals to the Chorus to defend him, but the Clouds say he deserves his punishment for trying to cheat his creditors. Furious, Strepsiades gets a torch and sets fire to The Thoughtery - they have richly deserved their fate for their blasphemies.

Comment

The inversion of the father-son relationship is a vestige of the rebirth and rejuvenation motifs of the old phallic rites. The Sophists are typified as teaching oratorical skills to ensure victory at court, whether justly or not. The caricature of Socrates is identified with this disruptive and pernicious system. The real Socrates was neither an unscrupulous orator nor a superficial Sophist. He and his disciples did share a common life of poverty in order to devote their time to philosophy, but not to the trivial subjects mentioned in the play.

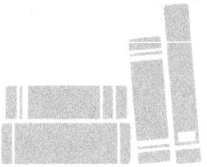

ARISTOPHANES

THE WASPS

BACKGROUND

Under the pseudonym of Philonides, Aristophanes produced *The Wasps* at the Festival of Lenaea. The **theme** is the contrast between youth and age, and includes a **satire** on abuses of Athenian legal procedure. It is better written than *The Clouds,* for the **satire** and the humor are more obliquely presented.

CHARACTERS

Philocleon: "Cleon-lover," an old Athenian.

Bdelycleon: "Cleon-leather," Philocleon's son.

Sosias: Philocleon's slave.

Xanthias: Philocleon's slave.

Boys

Dogs

A Guest

A Baker's Wife

An Accuser

Chorus Of Wasps

PROLOGUE

Two slaves, Xanthias and Sosias, are trying to stay awake in order to guard Philocleon. Their master is on guard on the roof, Xanthias explains to the audience, and they keep watch on his father, Philocleon so that he cannot come out. Philocleon has a disease; he is addicted to jury duty. "He is so accustomed to hold the balloting pebble" that his three fingers are permanently pinched together. Afraid of not being on the jury, he goes before dawn to the Heliaea and is first on line. He is merciless and always draws the convicting line on the pebble. To ensure that he has enough pebbles, Philocleon's yard looks like a beach. His son, Bdelycleon, has tried to persuade him, had him bathed and purified according to ritual, and forcibly taken him to the temple of Asclepius on the island of Aegina to be healed. But Philocleon managed to escape and arrive back in Athens for jury duty before dawn. Now Bdelycleon has his father locked inside the house with a net around it.

> Comment

The Athenian Dicasteria (law court) was composed of ten dicastae (juries) of five hundred qualified citizens each. They tried civil and criminal cases, and a complicated system of legal procedure made bribery impossible. During the Peloponnesian War, only the old men were left in Athens, and they received three obols for daily jury duty. Perhaps the unemployment, poverty, and the bitterness of old age made them such irascible condemners rather than impartial jurists.

Philocleon tries to escape by climbing out the chimney but his son forces him back down. He then tries to break down the door - it is necessary that he go judge, otherwise Dracontides will be acquitted - but the slaves put their weight against the door. Thwarted he asks his son to let him sell his ass. To expose the excuse, Bdelycleon brings out the ass, but it is sluggish and slow-moving. Philocleon is acting like Odysseus and clings to the ass's belly. Bdelycleon drags his father back inside. As they pile rocks at the door a brick falls on Xanthias. The father is acting like a rat and creeping beneath the tiles of the roof. Bdelycleon wonders why the other jurymen are late in coming to get his father: they usually come in the middle of the night in order to be first on line for jury duty. Xanthias suggests chasing them off with stones when they arrive, but Bdelycleon warns that "this class of old men, if irritated, becomes as terrible as a swarm of wasps. They carry below their loins the sharpest of stings, with which to prick their foe; they shout and leap and their stings burn like so many sparks."

> Comment

In the Odyssey, IX, Odysseus escapes from Polyphemus, the Cyclops, by hiding underneath a sheep when Polyphemus let

PARODOS

The old men enter, disguised as wasps. They want to hurry to the court, "for the case of Laches comes on today, and they all say he has embezzled a pot of money. Hence Cleon, our protector, advised us yesterday to come early and with a three days' stock of fiery rage so as to chastise him for his crimes." They wonder why Philocleon is not ready. Perhaps the acquittal of an accused man the day before so distressed him that he is in bed with a fever.

Comment

Aristophanes indicates that the jurors are not really interested in trying a case and following justice. They are more concerned with convicting every one brought before them. Like wasps, they are more desirous of harm.

AGON

Inspired by his friends, Philocleon attempts a new dodge while his son sleeps. Even though he is toothless, he gnaws through the nets. He fears his son, and if misfortune overtakes him he advises the wasps to bury him beneath the bar of the tribunal. Bdelycleon, nevertheless, wakes up and catches his father climbing down a rope. The Chorus of Wasps feel their sharp stings stiffening in anger and come to the old man's aid. Bdelycleon and the slaves drive off the wasps with blows and smoke. They argue from a distance, and the battle eventually becomes an argument between

Philocleon and Bdelycleon. Bdelycleon finally convinces the wasps that the demagogues are exploiting the jurors. They pay the jurors for attending the Heliaea and thus have people ready to do their will. Bdelycleon persuades his father to hold tribunal inside the house instead of going to the public courts. Philocleon's first case is that of Labes, the dog, who just ate a whole Sicilian cheese. But the trial keeps getting interrupted while Philocleon searches for a bar, the voting urns (Bdelycleon brings out some pots), and the water clock (Bdelycleon tells his father to use the chamber pot). Then Bdelycleon brings out the accused dog and another dog who will act as the accuser. Philocleon intends to convict the dog, but Bdelycleon calls witnesses for the defendant's side - a plate, a pestle, a cheese knife, a brazier, a stew-pot, and other half-burnt utensils. He praises the dog's abilities and tricks his father into acquitting the dog. Philocleon faints when he finds out that he acquitted someone.

And so I have charged my conscience with the acquittal of an accused being! What will become of me? Sacred gods! forgive me. I did it despite myself; it is not in my character.

Comment

The "disease" of jury duty is a mania to convict those on trial. The "disease" is so pronounced that it affects the juryman's health. An acquittal makes him ill, and Aristophanes points out the evils of contemporary legal practice.

PARABASIS

The Chorus reminds the audience of its ill-treatment of the poet, despite the many services he rendered to the Athenians.

In particular, Aristophanes reproaches the audience for its poor treatment of *The Clouds* the year before. Aristophanes then praises the old men for their courage in battle long ago, for nothing is more to be feared than the Attic wasp. Then the Chorus explains why they are dressed as wasps and attacks the lazy and effeminate citizens of the time.

Episode I

Philocleon and Bdelycleon emerge from the house. Bdelycleon tries to dress his father like a gentleman and teach him how to "imitate the easy effeminate gait of the rich." When Philocleon talks to the rich, he should discuss realities and tell some dignified story or some deed of daring from his youth. Philocleon, however, is recalcitrant. Then they hurry off to dine with Philoctemon.

Comment

This play deals with the father-son relationship more directly than *The Wasps*. Here, the son makes his father more modern and up-to-date in accordance with the ideals of youth. Bdelycleon tries to make his father a modern gentleman, with what results we shall soon see.

STASIMON I

The Chorus reviews the cleverness of several men. The wasps also explain that their reconciliation with Cleon is only to deceive him.

Episode II

Xanthias enters and tells the Chorus of the disastrous party. Philocleon got very drunk and behaved insolently. He insulted all the guests with gross jokes and reeled off "a thousand of the most absurd and ridiculous speeches." Philocleon enters, thoroughly drunk and carrying a torch, with a naked flute girl. A guest following him threatens to summon him to justice the next day. Feeling young, he offers the girl a place in his home:

> **You will play with me, you will laugh heartily at me as you have done at many another man. And yet, if you would not be a naughty girl, I would redeem you when my son is dead, and you should be my concubine, my little one. At present I am not my own master; I am very young and am watched very closely. . . . But here he comes running toward us. But be quick, don't stir, hold these torches. I am going to play him a young man's trick, the same as he played me before I was initiated into the mysteries.**

Bdelycleon arrives, and, after a comic scene in which he points out the parts of the girl's body and his father explains them as parts of a torch, a baker's wife enters to bring a complaint against his father. Philocleon knocked over her basket of loaves, worth fourteen obols. Philocleon mocks her with a tale from Aesop, and she leaves to get a summons. Another enters to summon Philocleon for his outrages. When he begins to tell obscene stories, the accuser leaves also to obtain a summons against Philocleon. Bdelycleon finally carries his father into the house by force.

STASIMON II

The Chorus points out Philocleon's happiness. Formerly he had frugal habits and a very hard life, but now he has adopted the ideas of others and knows nothing but the pleasures of ease. The Chorus also praises Bdelycleon's filial tenderness and tact.

EXODOS

Xanthias comes out of the house and reports that old Philocleon is "spending the night dancing the old dances that Thespis first produced on the stage." He even wants to take on the modern tragedians and prove that they are old dotards. Philocleon comes out dressed as Polyphemus and dances a grotesque **parody** of Euripides' style. He issues a challenge to the tragic poets to compete with him in dancing. Just then, the three sons of Carcinus enter, dressed as crabs, and begin to dance wildly with Philocleon. The Chorus urges the children on, for here "comes your famous father, the ruler of the sea, delighted to see his lecherous triarchoi." As for them, they will not join the dance, "for never a comedy yet was seen where the Chorus finished off with a dance."

Comment

The rebirth or rejuvenation motif of the phallic rituals of springtime is again observed in Aristophanes' play. The old Philocleon is behaving like a passionate young man. Aristophanes manages to slip in another **parody** of Euripides, this time for dancing style. At the end Aristophanes makes a pun on the word triarchoi, meaning "three kings," with the word triorchoi, "having three testicles" or being more virile.

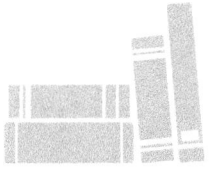

ARISTOPHANES

PEACE

BACKGROUND

Aristophanes' *Peace* won second prize at the Feast of the Great Dionysia in 421 B.C. The play was written hastily, for the peace negotiations, conducted by Nicias, were only shortly before seen to be heading toward a successful conclusion. As drama, *Peace* is weak because it lacks a good plot structure and any real conflict which would intensify the agon. But it is delightful and spontaneous in its humor and warmth.

CHARACTERS

Trygaeus: "The Crop Grower," an honest vine grower.

Trygaeus' Slaves

Trygaeus' Daughters

Hermes: The Messenger of the gods.

War

Tumult: War's lackey.

Hierocles: A soothsayer and oracle.

A Sickle-Maker

An Armorer

Lamachus' Sons

Cleonymus' Son

Chorus Of Farmers

Peace

Opora: "Harvest" in Greek.

Theoria: "Sacred Embassy" in Greek.

PROLOGUE

Two of Trygaeus' slaves are in front of the stable, one of them kneading dung cakes and the other throwing them into the stable to a dung-beetle Trygaeus is keeping there. The slaves complain of the odor and the dung-beetle that wallows in its food. Certainly Aphrodite or the Graces didn't "let this monster upon us." "No doubt Zeus, the God of the Thunderclap" did it. The second slave explains to the audience that his master is tired of trying to secure peace through customary legislation, and has gone directly to Zeus in his appeal. He even made ladders "and so clambered upwards towards heaven; but he soon came hurtling down again and broke his head." Now he has this huge beetle with which he hopes to fly straight to Zues. Trygaeus then flies out on the dung-beetle. He plans to fly up to Zeus, but the slaves and his young daughters try to persuade him not to. The daughters worry that the beetle might fall into the sea, but Trygaeus, exposing his phallus, replies that he has a rudder and the beetle would be his boat. The daughter finally warns him not to fall off and become crippled; then he would be a fit subject for Euripides and his tragedies.

Trygaeus finally arrives at the home of Zeus. Hermes calls him an impudent, shameless rascal, and demands to know the visitor's name. Trygaeus replies that he comes from the Athmonian deme, "a good vine-dresser, little addicted to quibbling and not at all an informer." Hermes tells him that Zeus is not here;the gods have moved away because of their wrath against the Greeks. They gave War the house and told him to do with the Greeks as he pleases. "Then they went as high up as ever they could, so as to see no more of your fights and to hear no more of your prayers. . . . Because they have afforded you an opportunity for peace more than once, but you have always preferred war." Hermes doubts that the Greeks will ever see Peace again, for War has cast her into a deep pit. War has also got a large mortar and he wants "to pound up all the cities of Greece in it."

War comes out of the house, and Hermes flees while Trygaeus hides. War pours ingredients representing Prasiae, Megara, and Sicily into the mortar, and then adds some Attic honey. Since he forgot to bring his pestle yesterday when he moved in, he sends his servant Tumult to Athens to get a pestle. Tumult soon returns, for the Athenians lost their pestle. War sends Tumult to Sparta, but they too have recently lost their pestle. War goes back inside to make a pestle for himself, and Trygaeus comes out of hiding. Now is the time, he declares, for all Greeks to come and dig Peace out of the pit.

Comment

The hero rides to Olympus on a disgusting dung beetle (cantharus). It is first a Pegasus and then metamorphosed into a hippocantharus, which gives the dung beetle a mythological stateliness out of keeping with its nature. But Zeus appreciates it enough to use it to draw his chariot, thus endowing it with a heroic, divine stature if not grace. Zeus the Thunderer in Greek is Zeos Kataibates. The elision of Zeos with the epithet creates the word, skataibates, a word that **rhymes** with the original concept of thunderclap.

War indiscriminately mixes ingredients of cities friendly and hostile to Athens, for the Peloponnesian War is panhellenic in its destruction. Trygaeus' appeal for peace is also panhellenic, for all Greek farmers unite to restore peace to their land. The farmers were those most affected by the war. They had to flee their ravaged fields and settle in the cities where they suffered from poverty, bad housing, and unemployment.

PARODOS

The Chorus of laborers and farmers from the various Greek states enters. They are zealous and in a hurry to rescue Peace.

AGON

They shout in their exuberance, and Trygaeus keeps warning the Chorus to be quiet lest War hear them. It is not yet time for joy - wait until Peace is freed. Hermes returns and demands to know what they are doing. They will die; he must inform Zeus because he has decreed death for whoever is caught freeing Peace. The Greeks will offer sacrifices to Hermes the Liberator and load him with benefits, if he allows them to free Peace. Softened by the bribes, Hermes not only permits the digging of Peace out of the pit, but even supervises the Greeks. The work proceeds with all the efficiency and zeal of the Keystone Cops. The Boeotians are only pretending; Lamachus is sitting in the way; the Argives do not help, "they have done nothing but laugh at us for our pains while they are getting gain with both hands"; the Laconian farmers pull with vigor, but their armorers impede them; the Megarians are pulling hard, but they are so famished that they accomplish nothing; some Greeks pull one way and others another; and the Athenians are not well placed for pulling. "There you are too busy with law suits."

Finally, with only farmers working, Peace is drawn out of the pit along with Opora and Theoria. The goddess smells sweet and a gentle fragrance comes from her bosom, not the smell of a soldier's knapsack or the belching of onions. "This lovable deity has the odor of sweet fruits, of festivals, of the Dionysia, of the harmony of flutes, of the tragic poets," and many other productive and enjoyable things. The Greeks hail their beloved deity and ask Hermes why Peace was lost to them. Hermes explains that it began with Pericles, whose Megarian decree started the war. Towns subject to Athens began to rebel and plotted with Sparta against her. The demagogues in Athens drove away Peace each time she reappeared in answer to the wish of the country. The author of all this woe was the tanner. Peace then ask Hermes to ask about the various people who were in Athens before, but they are gone or changed into others. Finally, Hermes instructs Trygaeus to take Opora for a wife in the country and Theoria to the Senate.

Comments:

Aristophanes satirizes the Greeks' inability to work with one another, even for peace. The tanner is a reference to Cleon's occupation before he became the bloodthirsty, warmongering ruler of Athens. Hermes' explanation for the war's start is, as in *The Acharnians,* weak and trivial.

PARABASIS

The Chorus reports to the audience that "if it be right to esteem the most honest and illustrious of our comic writers at his proper value, permit our poet to say that he thinks he has deserved a glorious renown." He has removed low buffooneries from comedy and built up a great art. And he has boldly attacked great men and not obscure ones. The first semi-chorus begs the muse to bring Peace, and attacks Carcinus and his sons - they are "machine-made poets." The second semi-chorus extends the attack to others.

Episode I

Trygaeus enters limping from his long trip. He is accompanied by Opora and Theoria. A slave comes out of the house and asks his master if he saw any other men in heaven. Trygaeus answers that he saw the souls of three dithyrambic poets "seeking to catch some lyric exordia as they flew by immersed in the billows of air." He also verifies that men are turned into stars after death. Trygaeus tells the slave to take Opora into the house and to prepare for the nuptials. After the Chorus tells Trygaeus how happy he will be, the slave reappears and announces that Opora and the preparations are ready. All that is lacking is the groom's sex organ.

Trygaeus leads Theoria to the Senate. She removes all her clothing and the Senators are all too eager to take her. They begin a feast of celebration and sacrifice a sheep. They pray to Peace to come like an honest woman and "cause the Greeks once more to taste the pleasant beverage of friendship and temper all hearts with the gentle feeling of forgiveness." They also request that crops and game be plentiful. Hierocles, the "oracle-monger from Oreus," appears and calls them idiots for sacrificing to Peace, Hierocles tells them that it is impossible to stop the war: the gods forbid it until the Golden Age returns and the wolf shall sleep with the sheep. Hierocles tries to get a share in the feast of the burnt offerings, and is chased away.

STASIMON I

The Chorus sings an ode praising the joys of peace and the plenty of the harvest. Instead of watching a rascally Lieutenant, the Chorus prefers "to see the Lemnian vines beginning to ripen. . . . Likewise I love to watch the fig filling out."

Comment

It is only when Peace's associates are made sensually attractive that the Athenian Senate is willing to accept her. The sweet smells of Peace contrast with the odors of the dung beetle, during the period of War.

The Golden Age is a persistent **theme** in literature from Homer to the present. It is set in a lovely place (locus amoenus or paradisos) of Nature that is very beautiful and fertile. It is usually linked with the reign of Saturn and the Elysian Fields. Its Christian counterpart is the Garden of Eden before Adam's Fall, when all Nature lived peacefully and harmoniously. Since it is impossible that the Golden Age return, it is impossible that Peace be established.

The fig is a reference both to the plant and to the male organ, thus fusing the fertility and phallic aspects of comedy's ritual origins.

EXODOS

Trygaeus comes out of the house and gets ready for the wedding feast. A sickle-maker and a cask-maker from the country come up to Trygaeus and give him some of their wares for presents. Since Peace is back, their business has improved. But an armorer, followed by manufacturers of various war materials, enters and complains that his business has declined. These war profiteers try to get some financial returns from Trygaeus, but Trygaeus implies that he will put them to excretious uses and insults the profiteers. They leave and their places are taken by Lamachus' two sons, who sing war songs. Trygaeus orders them to leave, then orders the feast to begin. He brings Opora out of the house and joins the Chorus in singing the Hymen Hymenaeus. The Chorus carries Trygaeus in triumph, while he sings, "You shall have a fine house, no cares and the finest of figs." The Chorus responds that "the bridegroom's fig is great and thick; the bride's very soft and tender." The play closes with Trygaeus' exhortation for his friends to feast.

Comment

The gamos is a festival having associations with the fertility rites of the phallus. The bridegroom's "fig" is both vegetative and phallic, and presents the wish for fertility in the fields and the race.

ARISTOPHANES

THE BIRDS

BACKGROUND

The Birds was presented at the Lenaea, where it won second prize. Its **theme** has been variously interpreted as an escape to a utopia, a peace play, a political play, or just plain fancy. *The Birds* may contain elements of these motifs, but only partially and inconclusively. Between this comedy and *Peace* there is a six-year hiatus in our knowledge of Aristophanes: whether he wrote and what he wrote can only be conjecture. *The Birds*, however, is Aristophanes' longest play, certainly his most lyrical, and considered by some to be his masterpiece.

CHARACTERS

Euelpides ("Hopefulson"), and Pithetaerus ("Persuade Friend"): Two elderly Athenians, disgusted with life in Athens and the war, looking for an ideal place to live.

Trochilus: Epops' servant.

Epops: The Hoopoe (lapwing), once a mortal (Tereus), King of Daulis and husband of Procne, the Athenian princess.

A Bird

A Herald

A Priest

A Poet

An Oracle-Seller

Meton: A geometrician.

An Inspector

A Dealer In Decrees

Iris: The goddess messenger of the gods.

A Father Beater

Cinesias: A dithyrambic poet.

An Informer

Prometheus

Poseidon: A God of the sea.

Triballus

Heracles

Slaves Of Pithetaerus

Messengers

Chorus Of Birds

PROLOGUE

Two Athenians, Euelpides and Pithetaerus, are completely disgusted with life in Athens and determine on finding an ideal place to live. They decide to seek out the Hoopoe, a lapwing who had been metamorphosed from the mortal Tereus into a bird. The Hoopoe would be better than the Pythian oracle, for as a man he would be sympathetic and as a bird he could know the geography of the earth. Euelpides and Pithetaerus have a jay and a crow for guides. They come to a desolate country, where they knock on a rock and call for Epops, the Hoopoe. When the Epops' servant Trochilus suddenly appears, they defecate in fear and their guides fly away. When Epops comes out, they tell him that they seek him because he has all human knowledge as well as that of birds. "And hence we have come to you to beg you to direct us to some cozy town, in which one can repose." Epops suggests several cities, which are all rejected. Inquiring about the life of the birds, they learn that the birds have neither purses nor the unhappiness attendant upon money; their life is very much like a honeymoon. Pithetaeus has a happy idea: the birds can build a city between earth and heaven. In this way the birds can reign over mankind and cause the gods to die of hunger, for "when men sacrifice to the gods, unless the latter pay you tribute, you exercise the right of every nation towards strangers and don't allow the smoke of the sacrifices to pass through your city and territory." Epops approves and calls the birds to hear the plan.

Comment

The play presents a social utopia which, like all utopias, criticizes the vanities and follies of man. The only critical problem is that no one is sure what Aristophanes is satirizing. It is not really a peace play, and it does not directly attack Cleon, Socrates, or Euripides. In fact, one critic calls the play the "anatomy of nothingness."

PARODOS

One by one, the Chorus of Birds comes in. They are individually mentioned, and many are satirically compared to prominent contemporaries of Aristophanes. The Chorus leader asks why they were called. When Epops explains that two men are there who wish to live with the birds, the birds see the men only as enemies and begin to attack them.

Comment

The members of the Chorus come in individually. There is no ode until the call to attack the men, and that ode is very brief.

AGON

Epops steps in between the men and the birds and dissuades the birds from attacking. Pithetaerus and Euelpides argue the case for their plan, appealing to the birds' pride by saying that the birds had been the first creatures and "kings . . . of all that exists, firstly of me and of this man, even of Zeus himself. Your race is older than Saturn, the Titans and the Earth." The birds were even the original rulers of Persia, the Greeks, Egypt and Phoenicia. Now the birds have fallen from dominion; stones are thrown at them, they are sold, and they are roasted for food.

The plan of Pithetaerus and Euelpides is to build a walled city in the air. The gods will then have to restore the birds' dominion or they will not be allowed to pass through the sky to earth for their love-making. Men will have to sacrifice to the birds first, or the smoke from their sacrifices will not be allowed to ascend. The birds, moreover, can attack man's fields and animals. In the city there will be no temples, only trees and bushes. The birds are delighted and inspired by the Athenians' words. To enable the men to fly, the birds tell them of a root which makes wings grow. Procne appears and inspires some off-color comments on the part of Pithetaerus an Euelpides.

PARABASIS

While the men are out getting their wings, the Chorus tells the audience the history of birds and describes their great importance to mankind: they mark the seasons of the year, and are omens (and therefore, must they not be divine?). The Chorus invites the audience to become birds. "All that is disgraceful and forbidden by law on earth is on the contrary honorable among us, the birds." Men can beat their fathers and even become forefathers. Being a bird is also useful: a weary and hungry spectator at a tragedy can fly home for dinner and return. A bird can leave the theater to relieve himself and return to the play without dirtying his cloak. And finally, the wings facilitate adultery.

Episode I

Pithetaerus and Euelipes return with their newly acquired wings. With the assembly of birds they decide to call the city "Cloud-cuckoo-land." Euelpides is sent off to supervise the building of the city walls, while Pithetaerus and a bird-priest offer sacrifice to the bird-gods. A poet suddenly appears with verses composed in honor of the city. They give him a fur and a tunic, then drive the pest away. An oracle-seller arrives, seeking money, and he is chased out. Meton the surveyor, an inspector of ballot boxes, and a seller of decrees also arrive and are quickly beaten and sent off running.

STASIMON I

The Chorus states that mortals must address their sacrifices to the birds from now on. The birds proclaim laws protecting birds, since they are divine creatures now. They offer rewards to the judges for awarding first prize to this play.

Episode II

A messenger announces that the walls of the city are finished. They have been constructed entirely by the birds. A second messenger reports that a god sent by Zeus has passed through the gates and penetrated the realms of the air without the knowledge of the jays, who were on duty. Iris, the messenger goddess, flies by and is stopped by Pithetaerus. He accosts her and demands to know her identity, by which gate she entered the city, whether she had a permit to enter, and other questions that arouse Iris' indignation.

A herald arrives from the earth and awards Pithetaerus a golden garland. Cloud-cuckoo-land is admired by men; they are emulating its industry; and ten thousand are coming to immigrate. To receive the men, a servant is sent out for wings. Three immigrants arrive, seeking wings for their own selfish purposes. A father beater wants to follow the birds' law that a son may peck its father; he is persuaded to be a cock and go fight. A poet wants wings so he can gather songs in the clouds; when they ask him to form a Chorus of Birds, he leaves in a huff. An informer wants wings to assist him in spying on people so he can drag them to the law courts; he is whipped and sent away.

Comment

The gods are outraged at this new city in "Cloud-cuckoo-land," but the mortals seem too willing to join it. Euelpides and Pithetaerus have to drive away the very people from whom they were fleeing.

STASIMON II

The Chorus discusses the strange and wondrous things the birds see in their flights. There is a tree called Cleonymus which has no heart, is good for nothing, and is as cowardly as it is tall. In the springtime its buds are calumnies and in the autumn it strews the ground with bucklers instead of leaves.

Comment

Cleonymus was one of Cleon's minions, and an informer in a case from which he received profit on the confiscation of the victim's property.

Episode III

Prometheus enters in disguise, hiding from Zeus under an umbrella. He tells Pithetaerus that there is not a man that sacrifices to the gods. The gods are hungry and the barbarian gods threaten war against Zeus "if he does not open markets where joints of victims are sold," Zeus is going to sue for peace, but Prometheus advises Pithetaerus not to accept unless Zeus restores the scepter to the birds and gives him Basileia (Royalty) in marriage. Basileia is a general manageress to Zeus. She is "a very fine young damsel, who makes the lightning for Zeus; all things come from her, wisdom, good laws, virtue, the fleet, calumnies, the public paymaster and triobolus." Her husband will have almighty power. Prometheus leaves, still nervous about being seen by Zeus. The envoys Poseidon, Heracles, and Triballus (a barbarian god) arrive from heaven to treat for peace. The terms of Pithetaerus are accepted after a comic quarrel, and he leaves for the wedding.

Comment

After Pithetaerus has dealt with the mortals, he has to deal with the gods. The entire universe is affected by the creation of this utopia, whose serenity and peace does away with the need for gods and the baser occupations of humanity.

EXODOS

The Chorus sings of the triumph of birds. Pithetaerus returns with his bride, the Chorus hails the new rulers, and Pithetaerus and Basileia fly to the throne of Zeus.

Comment

The play is about the absurdities of mankind. The hero, Pithetaerus, lives up to the meaning of his name as a persuader and creates a new world with himself as ruler. The use of words and discourse satirized in *The Clouds* has become the hero of this comedy.

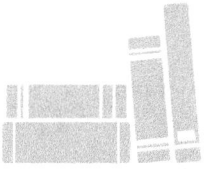

ARISTOPHANES

LYSISTRATA

BACKGROUND

Aristophanes' comedy about the Greek women's sex-strike for peace was produced at the Festival of the Lenaea in 411 B.C. We have no records about the awarding of the prizes, but this is one of the best comedies Aristophanes wrote. In a period when the Sicilian Expedition had been a dismal failure, Athens colonies were revolting, the Spartans were uniting with the Persians to control the Aegean, and there was a smoldering unrest within the city, Aristophanes put on his best peace play. This comedy is probably the most anthologized of all Aristophanes' works.

CHARACTERS

Lysistrata ("She who disbands armies")

Calonice ("Dried weed")

Myrrhine ("female genitalia"): Athenian women.

Lampito: A Spartan woman.

Anthenian Magistrate

Three Anthenian Women

Cinesias: An Anthenian, Myrrhine's husband.

Spartan Herald

Spartan Ambassadors

Anthenian Ambassadors

Chorus Of Old Men And Old Women

Chorus Of Athenians And Spartans

PROLOGUE

Lysistrata paces impatiently at dawn before the Acropolis. There is something important to consider and the women lie abed. Her neighbor, Calonice, enters, wondering what the meeting is all about. Lysistrata tells her it is about something very big which she has worked up at night and turned this way and that. Calonice remarks that it must be something very fine and slender for Lysistrata to have turned it so. Lysistrata informs Calonice that she intends to unite the women of Greece in order to save Greece. Myrrhine rushes in, soon followed by Lampito and ambassadresses from Corinth and Boeotia. Lysistrata asks them if they would help her end the war. Every woman makes great promises and they all brag about what they would do to secure peace, but when Lysistrata tells them it means giving up sex, they hesitate and refuse.

Lysistrata eventually convinces them that "we need only sit indoors with painted cheeks, and meet our mates lightly clad in transparent gowns." Their husband will certainly get excited and want to sleep with them. "That will be the time to refuse, and they will hasten to make peace, I am convinced of that!" If the husbands try to force their wives, Lysistrata counsels that they fight and give in with bad grace. There would be no pleasure in it for them, then, and they would tire of the game. Lampito argues that it would be impossible for the men to give up the war, so long as they have their ships and the treasury in the temple of Athena. Lysistrata has made preparations for this too; the older women will go to the Acropolis, as if to pray, and occupy it. To ratify their plan, the women take an oath. They bring out a large black bowl upside down and a flask of wine. The women place their hands on the bowl and swear, "I will have naught to do whether with lover or husband, albeit he come to me with an erection. I will live at home unbulled, beautifully dressed and wearing a saffron-colored gown to the end I may inspire my husband with the most ardent longings. Never will I give myself voluntarily, and if he has me by force, I will be as cold as ice and never stir a limb. I will neither extend my Persian slippers toward the ceiling, nor will I crouch like the carven lions on a knife-handle. And if I keep my oath, may I be suffered to drink of this wine. But if I break it, let my bowl be filled with water."

PARODOS

The Chorus of Old Men enters with wood and torches to burn out the old women who had seized the Acropolis. Before the

Propylaea, the entrance to the Acropolis, the Chorus leader urges the old men to place their torches in the pots of coals and then rush at the gate with a battering ram. While the old men are making their preparations to assault the Propylaea, the Chorus of Old Women comes out with pitchers of water. They have heard of the old men's plans and pray to Athene to be their ally and help them save Greece.

Comment

The dialogue of *Lysistrata* is filled with double meaning, and most every character takes the sexual meaning. In the Prologue, the flash of wine symbolizes the male sex organ, and the black bowl the female genitalia. Dionysus, as god of both fertility and wine, functions here in both aspects. The action of pouring wine (the final stage of fertility of the land) into the bowl parallels the ejaculation of sperm into the womb and contrasts with the sterility of the oath. Their oath promises them neither to enjoy intercourse nor to assume various positions for intercourse. The Parados continues the double entendres. The burning torches are an ironic symbol of the passions raging in old men's loins. Their attempt to batter through the gate is nothing else than a rape, and foreshadows the attempts of Cinesias later in the play.

PROAGON

The women and men argue and threaten one another. The women finally pour their water pitchers out on the men. An Athenian Magistrate enters, lamenting the license of the women. He admits that the men must share the blame for their conduct. A man goes to a jeweler, and another to a shoemaker, and asks them to work on their wives' catches. The Magistrate, too, is guilty - he has to get money for oarsmen for the fleet, but the women have locked the treasury. He calls for crowbars to force open the gates. Lysistrata opens the gates, and tells the Magistrate that they do not need crowbars, just common sense. The policemen attempt to arrest the women but they are beaten off.

Comment

The pouring of water on the old men to douse their sexual urges parallels the dampening of their husbands' passions to which the women have sworn. The Magistrate's **allusions** refer to the simple-minded invitations to adultery which men offer when they leave their wives alone. Yet Lysistrata will soon indicate that even adultery is impossible; there are no more men left in the city.

AGON

Lysistrata tells the Magistrate that the women have seized the treasury and will administer the money. The treasure is the cause of war and crime when the men manage it, therefore the women have decided to prevent the men from using the treasure. The Magistrate replies that they need the money to wage war. Lysistrata insists that this is the first thing - they mustn't wage war. The women, moreover, will save the men. At home, their husbands talked foolishly about war and told their wives to mind their own business. The men have committed the greatest folly of all - there are no more men in Athens. The women intend to "stir so amorous a feeling among the men that they stand as firm as sticks" and no longer desire war. To the Magistrate's question about how they would end the confusion in the Greek states and bring all the states together, Lysistrata answers with the image of a ball of wool.

> **First we wash the yarn to separate the grease and filth; do the same with all bad citizens, sort them out and drive them forth with rods - they're the refuse of the city.** Then for all such as come crowding up in search of employments and offices, we must card them thoroughly; then, to bring them all to the same standard, pitch them pell-mell into the same basket, resident aliens or no, allies, debtors to the State, all mixed up together. Then as for our Colonies, you must think of them as so many isolated hanks, find the ends of the separate threads, draw them to a center here, wind them into one, make one great hank of the lot, out of which the public can weave itself a good, stout tunic.

The Magistrate angrily retorts that the women don't have any share in the war. Lysistrata quickly answers that they bear children and then send their sons off to be soldiers. Furthermore, the women sleep alone. A man, no matter how old he is, can still get a young wife as long as he can get an erection. But women soon lose the bloom of youth and can find no husband. The women dress up the Magistrate as a corpse. He grumbles, and Lysistrata asks if he has not been laid according to custom. They will not forget to offer the proper sacrifices for him.

PARABASIS

The Chorus of Men fears a peril here; maybe the Spartans have stirred up the women. But the Chorus will be on guard and carry a blade hidden under myrtle boughs. The Chorus of Women reminds the Athenians that it doesn't matter if they are women; they can save Athena. The old men contribute nothing and endanger everyone's life. The women remove their garments. The Chorus of Men strip themselves and make ready to meet their enemies - the women. The women will stop at nothing, they are so cunning. "We shall see them buildings ships and fighting seafights, like Artemisia; and, if they want to mount and ride as cavalry, we had best cashier the knights, for indeed women excel in riding, and have a firm, fine seat for the gallop." The men and the women strip completely down and begin fighting.

Comment

All the Chorus of Old Men's remarks can be understood in several ways, as a fear of the unfeminine behavior of the women in waging peace, and sexually as an assuming of the man's position.

Episode I

Lysistrata comes out of the Propylaea with a gloomy face. She is downhearted; all the women want to go to bed with men, and are deserting. They are all thinking of excuses to go home. One woman comes out, for she wants to go home to protect her best wool from moths. All she wants to do is lay it out on the bed. Another woman wants to go home to strip her flax. A third wants to go out to find a midwife, even though she was not pregnant the day before. Lysistrata sees through all their subterfuges and makes them return to the Acropolis. There is an oracle that they shall conquer, and it would be shameful not to trust the oracle.

STASIMON I

The Chorus of Men and the Chorus of Women begin to argue, threatening to hit and kick one another. When one of the men goes to kick, a woman remarks that he's got a hairy "leg." When one of the women goes to kick a man, he remarks that he sees something. The woman replies, "You would see, for all my age, it is very well trimmed."

Comment

The dissension in the ranks of the united Greek women indicates that no one can do without sex. It is an artistic preparation for the next **episode**, in which Cinesias needs sexual satisfaction.

Episode II

Lysistrata appears on the Acropolis' walls and calls out that she sees a man approaching. He is Cinesias, Myrrhine's husband. Lysistrata instructs her that she must do everything to arouse her husband, but not let him in. Cinesias enters, obviously excited sexually, and tortured. He begs Myrrhine to come to him; he is stiff with desire. When Cinesias shows her their child, she comes down from the Acropolis. Cinesias tries to get his wife to come home to celebrate Aphrodite's mysteries, but she refuses until a peace treaty puts an end to the war. At any rate, she can lie with him for a little while. Myrrhine, in feigned shock, answers, "What, before the child?" Cinesias sends the child away with a slave. He wants them to make love in a cave and on the ground, but she leaves repeatedly for a mattress, a pillow, a blanket, perfume, and all the time leading him on. When

Cinesias promises that he will only "think about" a peace treaty, Myrrhine leaves him in a state of extreme desire and frustration.

The Chorus consoles Cinesias on his distress, but Cinesias prays that Zeus would sweep all the women up into the air and let them drop on the point of a man's erection. A Spartan Herald enters as Cinesias leaves. The Spartan is bent over in a too obvious state of frustration. The Athenian Magistrate thinks the Herald has a lance under his clothes, and if not, asks "why do you turn away like that, and hold your cloak out from your body? Have you got swellings in the groin from your journey?" The Herald reports that all the Spartan men have erections since Lampito has led the women on a strike. The Magistrate tells him that he "will urge our Senators to name plenipotentiaries from us; and to persuade them, why, I will show them my own tool."

STASIMON II

The Chorus of Men and the Chorus of Women make peace and help one another put their clothes on, but the women refuse to have intercourse with the men.

Comment

Cinesias' name derives from the Greek word "to move" and "to make love." The discomfort of the frustrated sex drives is having its effect on the men. Their erections are so bad that they can scarcely walk.

Episode III

Spartan Ambassadors come in, in as hard a state as the Herald. They wear long beards and look as though they were carrying pig pens between their legs. The Chorus of Old Men remarks that "the situation grows more and more strained! The intensity of the thing is simply frightful." They want peace, no matter which way it is spelled. Lysistrata comes out of the Acropolis. She reproaches them because all Greeks have common customs and a common religion, yet they fight against one another while the Persian is on the border. She also reminds them of the way they have helped one another in trouble in the past. The goddess Peace, completely and beautifully nude, is present at the discussion and distracts both sides. They finally exchange their oaths and pledges and depart.

STASIMON III

The Chorus of Women invite everyone to enter and choose what they will. "There is nothing so well sealed, you cannot break the seal and carry away the contents."

Comment

Aristophanes is constantly developing the **theme** towards its **climax**. With a presentation of the nude and beautiful Peace, the men find it impossible to continue the war. The Chorus of Women indicate their willingness to let the men have intercourse, after the treaty is made effective.

EXODUS

A Magistrate arrives and chases the Chorus off so that the Spartan envoys can leave the banquet. An Athenian leaves the banquet and indicates how pleasant the Spartans are, thus prompting the Magistrate to observe, "It's only natural, to be sure, for sober, we're all fools. Take my advice, my fellow countrymen, ours envoys should always be drunk." A Chorus of Spartans and one of Athenians come out, followed by Lysistrata and the women. They dance and invoke the gods in honor of their peace treaty.

Comment

In typical fashion, the Comedy ends in a gamos with a feast in which male and female are united. The Dionysiac ritual element is again presented in its twofold nature of human sexuality and vegetative fertility.

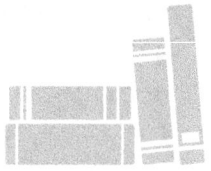

ARISTOPHANES

THE THESMOPHIAZUSAE

BACKGROUND

"The Women Celebrating the Thesmophoria" was produced at the Festival of the Great Dionysia, two months after *Lysistrata*. The Thesmophoria is a festival dedicated to Demeter, a vegetation goddess, celebrated in autumn by the women. The central **theme** of the play is a ridicule of Euripides, at whom Aristophanes had poked occasional gibes during his other plays. The precise motivation of this ridicule is Euripides' misogyny.

CHARACTERS

Euripides: The tragedian.

Mnesilochus: Euripides' father-in-law.

Agathon: A homosexual tragedian.

Agathon's Servant

Herald

Women

Clisthenes: A homosexual.

A Magistrate

A Scythian Policeman

Chorus of Thesmophoriazusae

PROLOGUE

Euripides and Mnesilochus enter on a matter of great and aggravating importance. Mnesilochus is something of a dunce and continually makes stupid comments or remarks. They arrive at the house of Agathon, to whom Euripides intimates Mnesilochus once made love. Agathon's servant stands in the doorway and pompously tells the audience to sit sedately silent. Agathon is going to . . . "make love," hints Mnesilochus. He is going to construct a drama. First he models it and then casts it into bronze . . . "and then sways his buttocks amorously," again interrupts Mnesilochus. The servant sees them, and Euripides tells him to call his master. Euripides must wait, however, until Agathon comes out, for in the winter he often comes out to let the sun excite his imagination. Euripides is worried, because the women are deciding today to execute a grievance against him since he mistreats them in his tragedies. Euripides wants to beg Agathon to go before the women at the Thesmophoria and stand up for him.

Agathon appears upstairs and sings parts from his tragedies. Mnesilochus is thrilled by his voluptuous and tender songs, and ask Euripides where this androgyny comes from. He asks Agathon if he is a man or a woman. Agathon replies that he is composing songs about women, therefore he behaves like a woman. Moreover, several celebrated tragedians were effeminate and successful. Euripides addresses Agathon, asking him to disguise himself as a woman and go to the Thesmophoria and plead Euripides' cause with them. Euripides cannot go because he is known and has a beard; Agathon is delicate, fair, and has a woman's voice. Agathon refuses to go, because it would look as though he were trespassing in order to rape the woman's Aphrodite. Mnesilochus mumbles that he means that he would want to be raped. Agathon still refuses, so Euripides intends to send his father-in-law. He begins to shave off the beard of Mnesilochus, who fidgets, and then shaves off his pubic hair. He dresses Mnesilochus, like a woman with Agathon's clothes and sends him to the Thesmophoria, first promising to save his father-in-law if anything happens to him.

Comment

Like *Lysistrata*, this play deals with the conflict between men and women, but here its treatment is more specific and literary - Euripides. The love element has also shifted, with many references to homosexual love instead of heterosexual love. The **satire** indicates the low state of tragedy. Agathon's appearance is managed by the eccyclema. Hairiness and beards were signs of virility, but Agathon's smooth shave indicates the effeminacy of contemporary tragedy. His rhetorical skill is a further indication of tragedy's decline in the substitution of external effect for content. This **episode** recalls *The Acharnians* when Dicaeopolis came to Euripides for help.

PARODOS

Mnesilochus sneaks into the Thesmophoria, where the Chorus of Women is gathered. A Woman Herald announces that the woman should pray to the Thesmophoria, Demeter and Cora, and to Plutus, Calligenia, Curotrophus, the Earth, Hermes and the Graces, for happiness. They pray that if there is anyone who injures and abuses women - listing the many possibilities and including Euripides - may the gods overwhelm them with their wrath.

AGON

The women begin to debate on what to do about Euripides. Because of his plays, the men always suspect the women and keep them locked up. One woman recommends that they get rid of Euripides by poison. Another woman agrees, pointing out that since Euripides has convinced everyone that there are no gods, she cannot sell religious chaplets of myrtle. The Chorus also agrees that the women should avenge themselves. Mnesilochus arises and pleads on Euripides' behalf: there are so many evils and deceits about woman that he did not make known. The women want to punish this betrayer of her own sex, while Mnesilochus continues to list female treacheries. Just before one woman begins to fight Mnesilochus, the pederast Clisthenes runs in disguised as a woman. He tells them that Euripides has sent one of his relatives to the meeting to hear the women's speeches and inform on them. He is a fairy and behaves like a woman, therefore he is their friend.

Mnesilochus is quickly discovered and guarded. His erection positively identifies him. The women guard him, while

Clisthenes goes to report to the Magistrate. To save himself Mnesilochus steals a woman's child, threatening to cut it open if he is not freed. The "child" is a wine skin, and Mnesilochus abuses the women as "you wanton, you tippling women, who think of nothing but wine; you are a fortune to the drinking-shops and are our ruin; for the sake of drink you neglect both your household and your shuttle." Mnesilochus rips open the "child" and lets the wine pour out. Recaptured, he worries about Euripides' rescuing him. He borrows a trick from Euripides' Palamedes and writes of his problems on wooden statues and scatters them right and left.

Comment

Aristophanes never stops mocking the women's desire for liquor, whether or not reality substantiates the insinuations. In Euripides' Palamedes the distressed victim wrote of his misfortunes on oars and cast them into the sea.

PARABASIS

The Leader of the Chorus addresses the audience, comparing the merits of men and women. The not unexpected conclusion is that men are inferior to women. In fact, a woman who has given birth to an illustrious citizen should have a place of honor at the festivals.

Comment

The "Parabasis" is loosely constructed and not typical of most "Parabases." It is incomplete and quickly written.

Episode I

Euripides still has not arrived to rescue his father-in-law, so Mnesilochus begins reciting lines from Euripides' Helen. The delaying tactic works, and Euripides enters playing the part of Menelaus. By reciting Helen's words, Mnesilochus indicates his predicament and begs "Menelaus" - whom he recognizes by the pot-herbs he carries -to carry him away quickly. The Magistrate arrives to punish Mnesilochus, however, and Euripides hides himself. The Scythian policeman accompanying the Magistrate ties Mnesilochus to a post in his women's robes so his crime will be known to passers-by.

Comment

Mnesilochus persists in playing the female, even though his true nature is known. That Euripides goes along with him is Aristophanes' slap at the lowness of Euripidean tragedy.

STASIMON I

The Chorus of Women sings hymns of praise to the gods to grant them victory and to lead them in their religious festival.

Episode II

Mnesilochus tries a new plan to get himself released. Euripides has returned disguised as Perseus and signaled Mnesilochus to play the part of Andromeda. He prays to the nymphs and to Echo, indicating that the Scythian closely watches him. He implores Euripides to save him. Euripides tells him he will not fail him, he will play the part of Echo. Everything that Mnesilochus says is repeated by Euripides - Echo, particularly the last few words. He also echoes the last words of the Scythian, but nothing works to free Mnesilochus. At last Euripides enters, dressed as Perseus. He tells the Scythian that it is Andromeda, the virgin, who is tied up. The Sythian lifts Mnesilochus' robe and exposes his sex organs; it is no woman. Euripides wants to free Andromeda, for he is aflame with love for the virgin and wants to join her on the bridal couch. The Scythian tells him he can make love to the old man there, but chases off Euripides when he tries to free Mnesilochus.

STASIMON II

The Chorus of Women prays to Pallas Athene, the protectress of Athens, to join them in their sacred orgies.

EXODUS

During the Chorus' ode, the Scythian policeman falls asleep. Euripides enters in a new disguise, that of an old bawd, and accompanied by a young flute girl and a dancing girl. The Chorus recognizes him, but Euripides offers to be reconciled with the women. He will never say anything ill of them in the future, if they will free his father-in-law; otherwise, he will expose all their pranks to their husbands when they return from the war. The Scythian wakes up, and Euripides has the girls disrobe to entice the Scythian. He leaves with the dancing girl, after commenting on the beauties of her body, and Euripides leaves with Mnesilochus. The Scythian returns after a while, for the girl is "not at all a prude and very obliging." He looks for the old bawd and Mnesilochus, but they have escaped. The Chorus tells him to hurry after Euripides and Mnesilochus, and points out the opposite direction from the one they took. The Scythian runs off in pursuit.

Comment

The misogynist Euripides has had to beg help from the women. In outlining what could have been said about the women, Aristophanes outdoes Euripides in exposing the deceits of women.

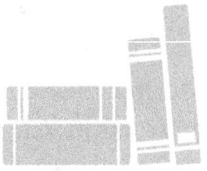

ARISTOPHANES

THE FROGS

BACKGROUND

Aristophanes' *The Frogs* was produced at the Festival of the Lenaea, where it won first prize. Its **theme** is literary and contains few bawdy elements, but it is not well-constructed or witty. Its popularity is more likely based on its inoffensiveness to prudes than on its artistic merits.

CHARACTERS

Dionysus: The god of fertility and wine, who disguises himself as Heracles to get Euripides back from Hades.

Xanthias: Dionysus' slave.

Aeschylus, Euripedes: The tragic playwrights, in Hades.

Heracles: Famous hero of the "twelve labors" who, as one of his labors, brought back Cerberus (the three-headed dog) from Hades.

Pluto: King of the underworld, which is called Hades.

Charon: Boatman of dead souls into Hades.

Aeacus; A judge of the dead.

Pluto's Servant

Corpse: A corpse on his way to his funeral who refuses to carry Dionysus' luggage.

Persephone's Maidservant

Landlady: Landlady of an inn in Hades to whom Heracles owed money.

Plathane: Her servant.

Chorus Of Frogs: They sing rowing songs when Dionysus crosses the river Styx.

Chorus Of Initiated Persons: Initiates into the Eleusinian Mysteries.

PROLOGUE

Dionysus, the god-patron of tragedy as well as of fertility and the vine, deeply feels the loss of Euripides, who recently died. His desire to see Euripides is so great that he decides to go down to Hades and bring Euripides back to earth. Appropriately, he chooses a disguise of Heracles. Dionysus enters incongruously wearing the lion skin and carrying the club of Heracles over the yellow robe of tragedy. With him is his servant Xanthias, riding a donkey carrying an enormous load of baggage. They knock at the door of Heracles' house, where, to Heracles' great amusement, Dionysus asks directions for getting to Hades. He has developed a great craving to have Euripides back on earth again, and he consults Heracles because he has been there and back. He wants Euripides instead of Sophocles, because Sophocles was content with the gods, but Euripides was not. Euripides is thus more likely to give Pluto the slip. Heracles suggests three quick ways to get down to Hades - hanging, drinking hemlock, or jumping off a high tower. Heracles tries to frighten Dionysus off by emphasizing the horrors to be encountered. Dionysus insists, and Heracles tells him that the Initiated at the door to Hades will tell him all he desires to know. The baggage is heavy, and Dionysus tries to get someone to carry it down to Hades for him. He stops a funeral procession, trying to get the dead man to help with the baggage, but the fee the man wants is too large. Dionysus and Xanthias finally come to the lake surrounding Hades and meet Charon, the ferryman. Charon refuses to take slaves unless Xanthias won his freedom in battle. But Xanthias had sore eyes at the time and did not fight. Xanthias has to walk around the edge of the lake and Dionysus is made to row.

Comment

The ubiquitous atmosphere of death is appropriate in a period of worsening Athenian military affairs. After the Battle of Arginusae, six months earlier, all the slaves who fought in the battle had been freed and given citizen status. Xanthias did not fight because he claimed eye trouble, a common enough illness in the past but more common during draft calls. *The Frogs,* then, is a somber play with political implications in addition to the literary **theme**. The literary theme includes other **allusions** to the theater besides the debate between Aeschylus and Euripides. Dionysus pays two obols to enter the boat, the admission fee to the theater, instead of the usual one obol.

PRO-PARODOS

The Chorus of Frogs is heard off-stage, singing "Coax, coax, coax, brekekekex coax," setting the rhythm for the rowing. Dionysus is heard complaining that he is sore and getting blisters.

PROAGON

On the other side, Xanthias rejoins his master, and they are both terrified by the monsters of Hades. Dionysus seeks protection from the priest sitting in the place of honor in the audience. Hearing music approaching, Dionysus and Xanthias crouch down to watch and listen.

Comment

The priest of Dionysus had the seat of honor, front row center, during the festival. The trip to the underworld is an established literary motif, found in the Odyssey, the Republic, the Aeneid, and the Divine Comedy, among many others. Dionysus' descent is part of his function as vegetation god; when the plants die in autumn they go beneath the earth to wait for the spring. Demeter functions similarly as a mythic explanation of this death of crops.

PARODOS

A Chorus of Initiates in the Eleusinian Mysteries enters. They sing to Dionysus, dance, and make satirical thrusts at corrupt persons and practices in contemporary Athens.

> Comment

The Eleusinian Mysteries comprised a Dionysian cult on the island of Eleusis which promised a happy life in Hades to its members. A secret organization, nothing is definitely known of its precepts or practices.

AGON

Dionysus and Xanthias join the dance and find out from the Chorus where Pluto's palace is. Aeacus, a judge of the dead, is Pluto's servant and opens the door of the house. Dionysus announces himself as Heracles, and Aeacus threatens him with torture by the monsters of Hades for the theft of Cerberus. Xanthias chides Dionysus for cowardice, and Dionysus says that if Xanthias wants to be a hero, he can put on Heracles' costume. Xanthias does and Dionysus becomes the servant. The maids of Persephone, Pluto's wife, come out and invite "Heracles" to a feast. Dionysus demands his costume back, but a landlady and her servant come on after the exchange and threaten Dionysus with lawyers because Heracles had left a huge bill at her inn when he was in Hades. Dionysus gives his costume back to Xanthias again. Aeacus returns with his two servants to arrest the dog-stealer. They overpower Xanthias, who tells them to interrogate (by torture) his boy, and if the police find Xanthias guilty, they can hang him. Dionysus reveals his true identity, but since doubt remains as to which is the god and which is the slave, both are whipped to find out the truth under torture. An immortal presumably feels no pain, and both try not to cry out, but finally do. Aeacus decides to take them to Pluto, saying, "He and Persephone will easily know you, being gods themselves."

PARABASIS

The Chorus advises the Athenians to do away with penal laws, for all Athenians stand equal. The Chorus also attacks the recent disenfranchisement of noble Athenian citizens and the elevation of unqualified persons to high position.

Comment

The parabasis' internal structure is changing, indicating Aristophanes' artistic flexibility and a sign of the decreased role of the Chorus in Middle Comedy. The comments satirize the recent enfranchisement of the slaves.

Episode I

Xanthias and Aeacus come out of the house, now good friends. They discuss the difficulties and pleasures of being servants. From inside comes the noise of a quarrel - Aeacus explains that Aeschylus and Euripides are arguing about first place in Hades. Aeschylus had held it until Euripides' death, but now the criminals have so loudly applauded Euripides' argumentative skill that he is claiming it. To settle the dispute, Pluto has ordained a trial in which each poet will argue his case. Dionysus is to be the judge. When Aeschylus and Euripides come out of the house, still railing at one another, Dionysus tries to quiet them and urges each to pray.

STASIMON I

The Chorus praises the Muses and looks forward to an exciting battle.

Episode II

Aeschylus prays to the gods, but Euripides refuses to do so. Euripides begins by attacking Aeschylus: his characters on stage have long silences; his choral passages are interminable; he uses long words and bombastic language; and he uses obscure language. Euripides says that in his own plays everything is made clear in the prologue; he uses realistic characters; he has taught men to examine all questions and to speak their minds freely.

Comment

Euripides' reputed agnosticism is played upon by Aristpohanes. Furthermore, Euripides, as leader of the new rhetorical style of writing tragedies, attacks Aeschylus for poor stylistic characteristics. It is noteworthy that his accusations do not include any concern for serious content.

Aeschylus replies, first asking Euripides on what particular ground a poet should claim admiration. Euripides answers, "If his art is true, and his counsel sound; and if he brings help to the nation by making men better in some respect." Aeschylus replies that Euripides' "realistic" characters are immoral and set bad examples. He justifies his own use of highly poetic language by holding it appropriate to lofty subject matter. A poet should hold truth enveloped in mystery, and not represent it or make it a play. The duty of a poet, Aeschylus says, is to teach. Euripides has trained almost every infant that crawls in the speechmaking arts, and this is the thing that has caused so much havoc and civil disobedience.

Comment

Aeschylus immediately gets down to the meaning of the debate - what is the function of the poet. Aeschylus indicates that his style is based on the needs of content and is not an end in itself. Euripides has concentrated on the less important and external matters of writing, and thus puts himself with the subversive influence of contemporary Sophists and orators, whose skill can make the worse reason appear the better.

STASIMON II

The Chorus urges the poets to continue arguing. The audience appreciates their paces and allusions.

Episode III

Each poet then quotes lines from his plays and the other attacks the statement and its language. In the famous "oil can" passage which follows, Euripides' prologues are made to appear repetitious and monotonous when Aeschylus shows that the phrase "Found his oil can gone" will complete the second half of many lines. Euripides retaliates by showing that Aeschylus' choral odes monotonously repeat the same rhythm. Aeschylus criticizes Euripides' songs by pointing out cheap effects and a triviality of content mixed with high comic style.

Dionysus calls for a set of balances, and each poet puts a line on each side. Aeschylus' side goes down. They try several more times, and Aeschylus always wins, for his "heavier" content lowers his side. Pluto comes out to ask who has won, but Dionysus has been unable to decide. He finally asks each poet how he would save Athens. Euripides, in general terms, recommends recalling the exiled rulers and throwing out those in power. Aeschylus recommends building a large navy. Dionysus decides in Aeschylus' favor, and when Euripides recalls Dionysus' oath to take him back, Dionysus quotes the line from Euripides' Hippolytus, "only my tongue swore."

STASIMON III

The Chorus remarks on the blessings of being intelligent. Because of his intellect, Aeschylus regains his home, benefits all who hear him, and stanches his country's fear. Philosophers like Socrates are foolish and absurd by neglecting the drama for scraping words on words.

EXODOS

Pluto bids farewell to Aeschylus, giving him swords and poison to use for sending certain Athenians to Hades. Aeschylus says that Sophocles should occupy his throne in Hades. By no means should Euripides be allowed that honor.

Comment

Dionysus has gone to Hades to rescue the tragic art so "that the city might be saved and present her choruses." In Hades, he realizes that Euripides' work disrupts the city and attracts criminals. True poetic art, on the other hand, should unite the individual and the city; it is a cohesive moral force. Aeschylus is thus the appropriate choice, for he is the poet of democratic Athens.

The **theme** of rejuvenation we have previously noticed is presented here as a rebirth. The return of vegetation in the spring is made to include the return of true Art. The Eleusinian Mysteries of Dionysus offered an emotional conviction in resurrection after death. The phallic origins of the Dionysiac ritual and comedy are beginning to change in a period of uncertainty to a more philosophic concept.

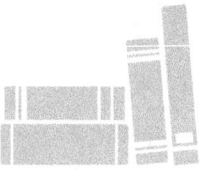

ARISTOPHANES

THE ECCLESIAZUSAE

BACKGROUND

"Women Attending the Athenian Assembly" was produced in 392 B.C., following a thirteen-year gap in our knowledge of Aristophanes' literary work. It is certain that he wrote during those years, but what and how much his output was we do not know. Also during that period, Athens lost the Peloponnesian War with Sparta, underwent a reign of terror under the Thirty similar to that following the French Revolution, and had democracy restored by Thrasybulus. In 399 Socrates was tried and executed, and there was a war with Corinth between 395 and 387. The "Golden Age" of Athens was certainly over, and within half a century the empire of Alexander would begin.

CHARACTERS

Praxagora: The leader of the women's revolution.

Blepyrus: Praxagora's husband.

Women

A Man

Chremes: "Coughing" or "snorting," a citizen.

A Citizen

Herald

A Girl

A Young Man

Three Old Women: Ugly prostitutes.

Praxagora's Maidservant

Chorus Of Women

PROLOGUE

Praxagora enters with a lantern to signal the Athenian women to begin their plot. Women begin to come in, dressed as men, in order to sit in the Assembly place. The women, moreover, have let the hair under their arms grow and have obtained beards. If a fairy could fool everyone into thinking himself a man, they should have no trouble. They rehearse their speeches, but they use so many womanly expressions that Praxagora delivers a mock oration, in which she proposes that the rule of Athens be turned over to the women. "Let us simply hand them the power, remembering that they are mothers and will therefore spare the blood of our soldiers; besides, who will know better than a mother how to forward provisions to the front? Woman is adept at getting money for herself and will not easily let herself be deceived; she understands deceit too well herself." The women make final adjustments in their costumes and go to the Pynx.

Comment

Praxagora's oration points out the vagaries of Athenian politics, the class struggles, and the people's loss of spirit in a depressing and changing period.

PARODOS

The Chorus of Women moves toward the Pynx, recalling the early days of the Assembly when citizens served for nothing. Now the citizen is as mercenary as the stonemason.

PROAGON

Blepyrus appears in front of his house wearing his wife's clothes. He has to go to the bathroom, and the only clothes he could find in the house are his wife's. As he squats in the alleyway, a neighbor looks out the window and talks with him. He, too, cannot find his clothes. After some comments on his constipation, Blepyrus is discovered by Chremes, who has come from the Assembly. Chremes tells him that there was a large crowd there, "and the folk looked pale and wan, like so many shoemakers." These pale shoemakers, moreover, outnumbered everyone else and voted that the women take over the city.

The speaker pointed out that men are untrustworthy and blabbermouths, but women are not informers, they do not bring lawsuits, and they do not hatch conspiracies. Thus, men and women will exchange places. Blepyrus fears that the women may force them to love-making, and compulsion takes all the fun out of it.

PARODOS II

The Chorus of Women marches back onstage. They make sure that no men are around and then remove their disguises.

AGON

Blepyrus comes out of his house and asks Praxagora where she has been. And why did she take his clothes? She replies that she had to go help a friend, but he says that she could have at least told him. He asks her if she has heard what the Assembly voted. Praxagora feigns ignorance, and Blepyrus informs her that the women rule over all public business. Praxagora is happy, for now there will be no more evil deeds and crimes. She believes her ideas are good, but fears "that the public will cling to the old customs and refuse to accept my reforms." Chremes tells her to have no fear: "love of novelty and disdain for traditions, these are the dominating principles among us."

Comment

Instead of convincing and changing Blepyrus, this scene points out the change in Chremes, who now favors the new government.

PARABASIS

Praxagora addresses the audience, explaining her plan: all property will be in common and all will have a share of everything. There will be one and the same condition of life for all.

Comment

In the fourth century Middle Comedy, the role of the Chorus declined, as indicated in the parabasis. It is the main character, not the Chorus, who speaks to the audience. Also noticeable in Aristophanes are the loss of boldness in his **diction** and the loss of attacks on statesmen in the speeches.

Episode I

Praxagora is interrupted by her husband, but she continues her explanation: all money, land, and private property will be common to all. Not only that, women shall belong to all men in common, and each shall beget children by any man that wishes to have her. The ugliest, furthermore, must be chosen or choose before the handsome men or pretty women choose. Violent beatings of old men will be stopped, Praxagora explains, because children will think the old men might be their fathers. Slaves will till the soil, and the men will only have to lie around the house. Thievery will vanish for everyone will have a common share. The law courts will be turned into dining halls, and "Athens will become nothing more than a single house." The women will also abolish the whores, so that they can have the first-fruits of the young men. "It is not proper that tricked-out slaves should rob free-born women of their pleasures. Let the courtesans be free to sleep with the slaves." Blepyrus follows Praxagora into the house, and Chremes goes to collect his goods.

STASIMON I

The Chorus does not sing an ode, but dances.

Episode II

Chremes brings his property on stage in preparation for redistribution. A Citizen, who is planning on first seeing which way things turn, mocks Chremes for obeying the new law. It is nonsensical and non-Athenian to give up goods. The Citizen is skeptical; he doesn't believe many will follow the new edict.

A Woman Herald summons everyone to the banquet. Chremes goes, but the Citizen plans to sneak into the banquet without having turned in his property.

STASIMON II

There is another interlude of dancing by the Chorus.

Episode III

At the houses of two prostitutes, an old whore and a young one argue. The old woman claims that she will get the lovers first, the young one argues that the only people who come to the old woman's house will be to carry her corpse out. A young man wants to enter the house of the young prostitute when the old one claims him under the new law. He is rescued by the young prostitute, but another old woman enters to claim him. A third and uglier hag appears to upset the claim, and the two women fight over him. They finally drag him off between them.

STASIMON III

Again there is no sung stasimon but a dance performed by the Chorus.

EXODOS

Praxagora's maid servant comments on how happy everyone is now. She stops Blepyrus on his way to dine and tells him that his mistress has bidden her to take him and some young girls to the banquet. "Some Chian wine is left and lots of other goods things. Therefore hurry, and invite likewise all the spectators whom we have pleased, and such of the judges as are not against us, to follow us; we will offer them everything they desire." The Chorus concludes the comedy with a reminder for the judges to award the play the prize, and for the audience to remember his comedy although it is to be played before the competitors' comedies. Then the Chorus follows Blepyrus and the maidservant out to the feast.

Comment

There is a tone of weariness observable in the play that is characteristic of periods after a "golden age" has left. It is a desire for rest and release from the labors of a life and a time that are no longer secure and convinced of life's meaning. All energy has gone; all that is left is the dragging out of existence. This tone is also noticeable in the late Golden Age of Latin literature and the late sixteenth century after the Renaissance.

ARISTOPHANES

PLUTUS

BACKGROUND

Plutus concerns the establishment of a Utopian community after the god Plutus (Wealth) regains his sight. The play was put on four years after *The Ecclesiazusae*. It is Aristophanes' latest and least humorous play of the eleven we have.

CHARACTERS

Chremylus

Cario: Chremylus' servant.

Plutus: God of Wealth.

Blepsidemus: Chremylus' friend.

Poverty

Chremylus' Wife

A Just Man

An Informer

An Old Woman

A Youth

Hermes: Messenger of the gods.

A Priest Of Zeus

Chorus Of Farmers

PROLOGUE

Cario complains that his master follows a blind man and abandons the worship of Apollo. Chremylus explains to this, the "most faithful and the most rascally of all my servants," that he used to worship the gods, yet remained poor and unfortunate. On the other hand, the sacrilegious, the demagogues, the informers, and rascals amassed wealth. He has, therefore, come to the oracle of Apollo to ask if his son should be a knave in order to be well off. The oracle's reply was that he should follow the first man he met, and this he is doing. They ask the blind man who he is, and after threatening him, he reveals that he is Plutus. He is blind because Zeus was jealous of mankind. When Plutus was young, he told Zeus that he would only go "to the just, the wise, the men of ordered life; to prevent my distinguishing these, he struck me with blindness! So much does he envy the good!"

If he had his sight, Plutus adds, he would shun the wicked and visit the good. But he knows that all men are wicked, and the good become evil when they become wealthy. Besides, Plutus fears that Zeus will be more angry if he should regain his sight, Chremylus, however, convinces Plutus that he is mightier than Zeus. The basis of Zeus' power is money, which he gets from Plutus. Sacrifices to Zeus are offered so that the suppliants can get money. Moreover, wealth is required to buy the sacrificial animals. Everything depends on wealth: slaves, prostitutes, merchants, the Persian King, the citizens of the Assembly, mercenaries, and writers. "In short, Plutus, it is through you that everything is done; you must realize that you are the sole cause both of good and evil." They arrive at Chremylus' house, and Chremylus orders Cario to call the other farmers in. Chremylus brings Plutus in to meet his wife and son, and indicates to Plutus that the strong point of his own character is moderation - Plutus should have no fear that Chremylus will be miserly or foolish with wealth.

Comment

Athens at this time was in a serious depression. No one had enough to eat, and the city could no longer maintain either medical service for the citizens or a Chorus.

PARODOS

The Chorus of Farmers rushes on stage, speeding as fast as old men can.

AGON

Cario tells the farmers that his master has brought Plutus to the house. They will all be wealthy. Chremylus comes out of the house and embraces his friends. Blepsidemus runs in; he has heard about Chremylus' wealth at the barber shop. He is Chremylus' friend, but he is suspicious about how all this wealth was acquired. Chremylus informs him that he has Plutus inside the house, but he is blind. They have to cure his blindness first. Blepsidemus suggests getting a physician in Athens, but Chremylus objects that "there's no art where there is no fee." They should bring Plutus to the temple of Asclepius.

A terrifying figure, Poverty, enters and scares the friends out of their wits. She wants to destroy them for seeking to banish her from every country. The friends decide to debate Poverty to prove the correctness of their action. Chremylus argues that it is right that the good be happy and the wicked miserable. If Plutus regains his sight he will make this so. "Can anything better be conceived for the public good?" All men will become honest, rich and pious. Poverty answers that all toil will be done away with and everyone will live in idleness. To Chremylus' retort that the slaves will do the work, Poverty states that no rich man would risk his life in the slave trade. All men will have to work, thus making their lives more wretched than they are now. No one will make furniture or perfumes. Chremylus rebuts her statement; Poverty gives man nothing but lice, hunger, rags, and bad food. Poverty answers that this is beggary, not poverty. "The poor man lives thriftily and attentive to his work; he has not got too much, but he does not lack what he really needs.... With me men are worth more, both in mind and body, than with Plutus. With him they are gouty, big-bellied, heavy of limb and scandalously stout; with me they are thin, wasp-waisted, and terrible to the foe."

In public life, modesty dwells with Poverty and insolence with Plutus, she argues. Orators who are poor are praised for their uprightness. "But once they are fattened on the public funds, they conceive a hatred for justice, plan intrigues against the people and attack the democracy." Chremylus asks why then does mankind flee from Poverty. She answers that children flee the wise counsels of their fathers, it is so difficult to see one's true interest. Chremylus refuses to be persuaded, even Zeus is rich and keeps his wealth. He awards the victors at the Olympic games only a wild olive garland. Finally, Chremylus chases Poverty off, but she remarks as she leaves that one day she will be recalled. Chremylus and Blepsidemus then hasten to bring Plutus to the temple of Asclepius.

Comment

Poverty points out, first, the private benefits, and second, the public benefits she confers. Everyone at this time was too acquainted with Poverty to believe her.

PARABASIS

As in *The Ecclesiazusae,* the Chorus does not sing but dances to the music of an ode.

Episode I

Cario tells the Chorus and Chremylus' wife that he has good news. They went to the temple of Asclepius and, after purifying themselves, consecrated sacrifices and made Plutus lie on the couch according to the rite. Asclepius came and cured Plutus. Plutus is now coming, followed by a happy throng of the poor, while the rich glower at him. The Wife goes into the house to get gifts of welcome for Plutus, and Cario goes to meet him.

STASIMON I

The Chorus dances to the music.

Comment

The Chorus' declining function is evident in their dancing. They do nothing but mark the change of scene and give the performers time to change. The slave's description of the healing of Plutus in the temple underscores the widespread hunger of the period. The priest of Asclepius creeps around at night while the suppliants sleep, and "consecrates" all the food offerings by stuffing them into his bag. The slave imitates the priest and steals food, occasionally breaking wind. The smell doesn't bother the Athenians (who are presumably used to this effect of an empty stomach), just the attendants of Asclepius.

Episode II

Plutus arrives, thanking and blessing the land. He blushes to think of the people he previously associated with while he shunned those who deserved his friendship. Chremylus' wife comes out to shower gifts of welcome on Plutus, but he tells her not to until they are inside. It is not proper that the poet should throw dried figs and dainties to the audience, since it is a vulgar trick to make them laugh.

STASIMON II

The Chorus dances.

Comment

Throwing figs into the audience seems to have been a commonplace trick which Aristophanes derides. It is one way of distracting an audience and keeping them entertained. Those who cannot reach the figs are amused at the antics of those who scramble and jostle for them.

Episode III

Cario exclaims how wonderful is luxury. A Just Man enters to thank the god for all his blessings. He wishes to dedicate his old cloak and shoes to the god; when he was poor, he had no friends, but now he has many. The Informer enters complaining that the god has caused him to lose everything. The Just Man thinks that all Greeks owe gratitude to Plutus, "by Zeus the Deliverer," for destroying these vile informers. The Informer claims to be an honest man and a good citizen, but, under the Just Man's questioning, it is learned that he is not a husbandman, a merchant, or a tradesman. The Informer says that he superintends public and private business, to which the Just Man adds that he sneaks in like a thief where he has no business. Cario strips the Informer of his cloak and shoes, and gives him the Just Man's old rags. This is what he deserves for "meddling with other folk's business and living at their expense."

| **STASIMON III**

The Chorus dances.

| Episode IV

An old woman enters dressed as a young girl. She complains to Chremylus that ever since Plutus made everyone rich her young lover has ignored her. Chremylus realizes that she is oversexed and, to get a lover, used to give gifts to the poor young man. While she complains, Chremylus makes sarcastic comments to the audience.

> Woman: Ah! friend, I am pining away with grief.
>
> Chremylus: You are rotting away, it seems to me.
>
> Woman: I have grown so thin, I could slip through a ring.
>
> Chremylus: Yes, if it were as large as the hoop of a sieve.

The Young Man enters, richly arrayed as though he were going to a festival. He insults the woman, she is so old. He doesn't want her anymore; she is so old she has been made love to by the thirteen thousand men in the audience. After more squabbling, the two enter the house to honor Plutus. Chremylus observes that "that old hag has fastened herself to her youth like a limpet to its rock."

STASIMON IV

The Chorus dances.

EXODOS

Hermes enters and knocks on Chremylus' door. He warns Cario that Zeus wants to punish them all. "Since Plutus has recovered his sight, there is nothing for us other gods, neither incense, nor laurels, nor cakes, nor victims, nor anything in the world." Hermes is hungry and asks for pity. He would be willing to leave the gods to stay with the humans. He would desert and find employment among men.

Cario: But how could we employ you here?

Hermes: Place me near the door; I am the watchman god and would shift off the robbers.

Cario: Shift off! Ah! but we have no love for shifts.

Hermes: Entrust me with business dealings.

Cario: But we are rich: why should we keep a haggling Hermes?

Hermes: Let me intrigue for you.

Cario: No, no intrigues are forbidden; we believe in good faith.

Hermes: I will work for you as a guide.

Cario: But the god sees clearly now, so we no longer want a guide.

Hermes: Well then, I will preside over the games ...

Cario: How useful it is to have so many names! Here you have found the means of earning your bread.

Cario and Hermes go into the house. A Priest of Zeus soon comes hurrying in and asks to see Chremylus. Since Plutus has recovered his sight, no one sacrifices to Zeus the Deliverer and the Priest is dying of starvation. There is not the smallest victim in the temple, only those who come to defecate. Chremylus suggests that the Priest take his share of those offerings.

The Priest ignores the remark and asks if he can stay with Chremylus. It is all right; Zeus is also there. Chremylus then calls out for everyone to assemble, so that they can install Plutus on the Acropolis. And he promises the old woman that her young man will return.

Comment

The play is essentially escapist. It offers a wish-fulfillment for wealth and luxury to the poor and hungry Athenians. Hermes had many functions as a god, but only one of them suitable for contemporary life, that of distracting the people by entertainments.

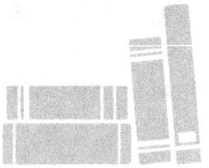

ESSAY QUESTIONS AND ANSWERS

Question: What is meant by the term "Old Comedy"?

Answer: The term is used to describe Greek comedy up to the end of the fifth century. The only examples to have survived are the first nine of Aristophanes' eleven extant plays.

Question: What are the main characteristics of Old Comedy?

Answer: Old Comedy strives to be as different as possible from tragedy. Characters are fantastic; the Chorus sometimes represents animals or inanimate objects; there is much obscenity; there is much political **satire**; personal attacks are made on famous contemporaries; and the **episodes** are not closely related to one another.

Question: What is the function of the Chorus in Old Comedy?

Answer: The Chorus in Old Comedy wears outlandish, colorful costumes in order to contribute to the spectacle. As animals or insects, they lend an element of absurdity. They frequently act as antagonists to the "happy idea" and must be convinced and won over. Their choral odes between **episodes** comment on the **theme** of the play. And, in the parabasis, they address the audience directly on behalf of the poet.

Question: What is satirized in *The Clouds?*

Answer: A caricature of Socrates and the Sophist school of philosophy are satirized. The historical Socrates is distorted by being made a Sophist and an advocate of fraudulent learning. Miserly old men and extravagant sons are also criticized, but the latter are viewed more indulgently.

Question: What other literary **genre** does *The Birds* resemble?

Answer: The utopian novel, play, or essay. A utopia is an ideal community, which in this play is founded by transforming men into birds and abolishing those parts of human society Aristophanes thought to be responsible for Athenian corruption.

Question: What occupations or activities is Aristophanes most opposed to?

Answer: Any activity which Aristophanes considered to be against the good of society he opposed. Generally, he was a conservative. He opposed abstract philosophy, oratorical persuasion, and the new scientific thought because he considered them to be destructive of traditional attitudes toward religion and morality. He was opposed to anyone who put the gaining of money above virtue or the good of society. Any form of personal cheating, public fraud, and political demagoguery was likely to become the object of ridicule in his harsh satires.

Question: What is the symbolism of the names of the main characters in *Lysistrata?*

Answer: Lysistrata, the leader of the women, means "she who disbands armies." Calonice is "dried weed," Myrrhine is based on the word for female genitalia and Cinesias comes from the same root as kinetic, and means "to move" and "to make love."

Question: What part does the Chorus of frogs have in *The Frogs?*

Answer: They only appear to sing the rowing song when Dionysus crosses the River Styx. The Chorus in the rest of the play is composed of Initiates into the Eleusinian Mysteries. The frogs' rowing chant is the basis of Yale's well-known yell.

Question: What is Aristophanes' attitude to the gods?

Answer: Aristophanes has a great respect for the old forms of religion; when he parodies the gods in his plays, he is following a traditional form of entertainment which was not regarded as disrespectful or sacrilegious.

Question: Why does Aristophanes object to Euripides' plays?

Answer: In *The Frogs* and other plays, Aristophanes attacks Euripides' plays for representing undignified characters who speak an undignified language, for being immoral, and for teaching subversive skills of argumentation to the rabble.

Question: How does Aristophanes' conservatism manifest itself in his plays?

Answer: Aristophanes praises the older forms of tragedy, the older forms of government, and the older forms of religion. He is suspicious of the new learning and the new oratory, linking them with homosexuality and disruptive speeches. He makes fun of innovations in government recently tried by Athens.

Question: What is the "happy idea" in Old Comedy?

Answer: The "happy idea" is a scheme by the leading character to improve his own lot or that of mankind. It is always tried out after a debate, and the second half of the comedy shows the idea in practice. Although the idea is ridiculous or impossible, it serves for both political **satire** and comic situations.

BIBLIOGRAPHY

GENERAL BACKGROUND

Aristotle, "Poetics," in Introduction to Aristotle, ed. Richard McKeon, New York: Modern Library, 1947.

Bowra, C. M., Classical Greece (The Great Ages of Man), New York: Time, Inc., 1965.

_____, The Greek Experience, New York: Mentor Books, 1957.

The Cambridge Ancient History, eds. J. B. Bury, S. A. Cook, F. E. Adcock, Vol. V (Athens: 478 - 401 B.C.), Cambridge: Cambridge University Press, 1953.

DeBurgh, W. G., The Legacy of the Ancient World, Vol. I, Baltimore: Penguin Books, 1953.

Hadas, Moses, A History of Classical Literature, New York: Columbia University Press, 1950.

Hamilton, Edith, The Greek Way to Western Civilization, New York: Mentor Books, 1957.

_____, Mythology, New York: Mentor Books, 1953.

Jaeger, Werner, *Paideia: The Ideals of Greek Culture*, tr. Gilbert Highet, Vol. I, New York: Oxford University Press, 1945.

Kitto, H. D. F., *The Greeks*, Baltimore: Penguin Books, 1957.

Livingston, R. W., *Greek Ideals and Modern Life* (Vol. V of The Martin Classical Lectures), Cambridge: Harvard University Press, 1935.

Nilsson, Martin P., *A History of Greek Religion*, tr. F. J. Fielden, 2d ed., Oxford: Clarendon Press, 1949.

Norwood, Gilbert, *Greek Comedy*, New York: Hill and Wang, 1963.

Ovid. *Metamorphoses*, tr. Horace Gregory, New York: Mentor Classics, 1960.

Rose, H. J., *Outlines of Classical Literature*, New York: Meridian Books, 1961.

Webster, T. B. L., *Greek Theatre Production*, London: Methuen, 1956.

TEXTS

Aristophanes, *Eleven Comedies*, tr. anon., New York: H. Liveright, 1928.

Aristophanes in English Verse, tr. Arthur S. Way, London: Macmillan and Co., 1927.

The Complete Greek Drama, eds. Whitney J. Oates and Eugene O'Neill, Jr., 2 vols., New York: Random House, 1938.

The Loeb Classical Library edition of Aristophanes in Greek and English on facing pages, tr. Benjamin B. Rogers, 3 vols., Cambridge: Harvard University Press, 1950.

CRITICAL WORKS

Allen, James T., *Aristophanes and the Pynx,* Berkeley: University of California Press, 1936.

Ehrenberg, Victor, *The People of Aristophanes: A Sociology of Old Attic Comedy*, 2d ed. rev., Oxford: Blackwells, 1951.

Lord, Louis E., *Aristophanes: His Plays and His Influence* (Our Debt to Greece and Rome series), New York: Cooper Square Publishers, Inc., 1963.

Murray, Gilbert, *Aristophanes: A Study*, New York: Russell and Russell, Inc., 1964.

Strauss, Leo, *Socrates and Aristophanes,* New York: Basic Books, 1966.

Whitman, Cedric H., *Aristophanes and the Comic Hero* (Vol. XIX of the Martin Classical Lectures), Cambridge: Harvard University Press, 1964.

www.ingramcontent.com/pod-product-compliance
Lightning Source LLC
LaVergne TN
LVHW011723060526
838200LV00051B/3005